Non-Governmental Development Organizations and the Poverty Reduction Agenda

The Non-Governmental Development Organizations (NGDOs) have, over the past two decades, entered center stage in their active participation in the social, political, and economic issues affecting both the developing and developed world. This book offers a highly stimulating and concise summary of the NGDO sector by examining their history and metamorphosis; their influence on the social, political, and economic landscapes of the "Northern" and "Southern" governments and societies. The author analyzes competing theoretical and conceptual debates not only regarding their contribution to the global social and political dynamism but also on the sector's changing external influence as they try to mitigate poverty in marginalized communities. This book presents NGDOs as multidimensional actors propelled by the desire to make a lasting change but constrained by market-oriented approaches to development and other factors both internal and external to their environment. While a lot of attention has been given to understanding international NGDOs like World Vision International, Oxfam, Care International, and Plan International, this book offers a critical analysis of grassroots organizations—those NGDOs founded and established by locals and operating at the deepest end of the development context.

This work will be of interest to students and scholars in a range of areas including Development Studies, International Organizations, and Globalization.

Jonathan J. Makuwira obtained his PhD at the University of New England (UNE) in October 2003. He is currently a Senior Lecturer in International Development at the Royal Melbourne Institute of Technology (RMIT) University. Prior to coming to RMIT he taught Peace Studies at UNE, and Comparative Indigenous Studies at Central Queensland University. He worked for the Ministry of Education in Malawi as a primary, secondary and teacher educator. He joined the Malawi Institute of Education in 1990 as a research officer, before joining the Council for NGOs in Malawi (CONGOMA) in 1998 as a Research Officer.

Routledge Global Institutions Series

Edited by Thomas G. Weiss
The CUNY Graduate Center, New York, USA
and Rorden Wilkinson
University of Manchester, UK

About the series

The Global Institutions Series has two "streams." Those with blue covers offer comprehensive, accessible, and informative guides to the history, structure, and activities of key international organizations, and introductions to topics of key importance in contemporary global governance. Recognized experts use a similar structure to address the general purpose and rationale for specific organizations along with historical developments, membership, structure, decision-making procedures, key functions, and an annotated bibliography and guide to electronic sources. Those with red covers consist of research monographs and edited collections that advance knowledge about one aspect of global governance; they reflect a wide variety of intellectual orientations, theoretical persuasions, and methodological approaches. Together the two streams provide a coherent and complementary portrait of the problems, prospects, and possibilities confronting global institutions today.

Related titles in the series include:

Trade, Poverty, Development (2013)
edited by Rorden Wilkinson and James Scott

The United Nations Development Programme and System (2011)
by Stephen Browne

Non-Governmental Organizations in World Politics (2011)
by Peter Willetts

Global Governance, Poverty, and Inequality (2010)
edited by Jennifer Clapp and Rorden Wilkinson

Non-Governmental Development Organizations and the Poverty Reduction Agenda

The moral crusaders

Jonathan J. Makuwira

Routledge
Taylor & Francis Group

LONDON AND NEW YORK

First published 2014
by Routledge
2 Park Square, Milton Park, Abingdon, Oxon OX14 4RN

and by Routledge
711 Third Avenue, New York, NY 10017

*Routledge is an imprint of the Taylor & Francis Group, an informa
business*

British Library Cataloguing in Publication Data
A catalogue record for this book is available from the British
Library

Library of Congress Cataloging in Publication Data
Makuwira, Jonathan.
Nongovernmental development organizations and the poverty
reduction agenda : the moral crusaders / Jonathan Makuwira.
    pages cm. – (Routledge global institutions series)
Summary: "This book offers a highly stimulating and concise
summary of the NGDO sector by examining their history and
metamorphosis; their influence on the social, political and
economic landscapes of the 'Northern' and 'Southern' governments
and societies"– Provided by publisher.
    Includes bibliographical references and index.
    1. Non-governmental organizations. 2. Poverty. 3. Economic
development. I. Title.
    H97.M338 2014
    362.5'5772–dc23
                2013022535

ISBN: 978-0-415-70443-4 (hbk)
ISBN: 978-0-415-70444-1 (pbk)
ISBN: 978-1-315-85770-1 (ebk)

Typeset in Times New Roman
by Taylor & Francis Books

Contents

Illustrations

Figures

Tables

Boxes

Foreword

The current volume is the eightieth title in a dynamic series on global institutions. These books provide readers with definitive guides to the most visible aspects of what many of us know as "global governance." Remarkable as it may seem, there exist relatively few books that offer in-depth treatments of prominent global bodies, processes, and associated issues, much less an entire series of concise and complementary volumes. Those that do exist are either out of date, inaccessible to the non-specialist reader, or seek to develop a specialized understanding of particular aspects of an institution or process rather than offer an overall account of its functioning and situate it within the increasingly dense global institutional network. Likewise, existing books have often been written in highly technical language or have been crafted "in-house" and are notoriously self-serving and narrow.

The advent of electronic media has undoubtedly helped research and teaching by making data and primary documents of international organizations more widely available, but it has complicated matters as well. The growing reliance on the Internet and other electronic methods of finding information about key international organizations and processes has served, ironically, to limit the educational and analytical materials to which most readers have ready access—namely, books. Public relations documents, raw data, and loosely refereed websites do not make for intelligent analysis. Official publications compete with a vast amount of electronically available information, much of which is suspect because of its ideological or self-promoting slant. Paradoxically, a growing range of purportedly independent websites offering analyses of the activities of particular organizations has emerged, but one inadvertent consequence has been to frustrate access to basic, authoritative, readable, critical, and well-researched texts. The market for such has actually been reduced by the ready availability of varying quality electronic materials.

For those of us who teach, research, and operate in the area, such access to information and analyses has been frustrating. We were delighted several years ago when Routledge saw the value of a series that bucks this trend and provides key reference points to the most significant global institutions and issues. They were betting that serious students and professionals would want serious analyses, and they were right. We have assembled a first-rate team of authors to address that market, and the titles—in print and electronic form—are selling well. Our intention remains to provide one-stop shopping for all readers— students (both undergraduate and postgraduate), negotiators, diplomats, practitioners from nongovernmental and intergovernmental organizations, and interested parties alike—seeking insights into the most prominent institutional aspects of global governance.

Non-Governmental Development Organizations and the Poverty Reduction Agenda: The Moral Crusaders

As we have argued elsewhere, the growing salience of non-state actors in world politics is one of the dominant explanations for the increased prominence of the framework of global governance rather than international organization.[1] Here we are referring to the sheer expansion in numbers and importance from both civil society (not-for-profit) and the market (for-profit), as well as transnational and transgovernmental networks of various types. That intergovernmental organizations, which figure prominently in this series, like the United Nations (UN) or the European Union or World Trade Organization no longer appear alone in the limelight on center stage for students of international organization was symbolized by the establishment of the Global Compact at the UN's Millennium Summit of 2000. Members of the private sector—both the for-profit and the not-for-profit species—were recognized as necessary partners for the world organization as the last and most formidable bastion of sovereign equality for its 193 member states. There is an ever more crowded governance stage. "Multi-level governance," "multiple-multilateralisms," and "multiple stakeholders" capture reality and are not merely academic jargon.[2]

A knowledgeable reader may protest that international nongovernmental organizations (INGOs) and transnational corporations (TNCs) have been with us for some time. The creation of anti-slavery groups in Britain and the United States at the end of the eighteenth century and early nineteenth century jumps to mind, or even the founding of the Sovereign Constantinian Order in 312 and the Order of St Basil the Great in 358. The British and the Dutch East India companies were chartered in the first years of the seventeenth century. Of course, the numbers of intergovernmental organizations (IGOs) have grown steadily since the public unions of the nineteenth century.

Again, however, the growth in the number and scope of intergovernmental and nongovernmental organizations makes the current situation distinct. Over the twentieth century, more than 38,000 international organizations were founded—a rate of more than one per day. More than 33,000 were founded after 1950, and almost half of all organizations created between 1900 and 1999 were established in the last two decades of the twentieth century.[3] The result, to borrow an image from the late James Rosenau, is a "crazy quilt" of authority that is constantly shifting; the current patchwork of institutional elements varies by sector, region, and time period.[4]

While an earlier book in this series focused on the advocacy and policy impact of NGOs,[5] their importance to the actual improvement of people's lives in developing countries is essential—both to the citizens of those countries and to our understanding of contemporary international relations. Hence, we are pleased to publish Jonathan Makuwira's in-depth look at the impact of both international and local nongovernmental development organizations (NGDOs).

A senior lecturer in international development at the Royal Melbourne Institute of Technology (RMIT) University, Jonathan Makuwira's current research involves urban poverty and NGDO intervention mechanisms in Malawi. His book *Basic Education in Malawi: Objectives, Problems and Perspectives* is partly derived from his experiences as an educator there.[6] He has also published numerous academic articles and book chapters on international development and education issues.[7]

We are pleased to publish his current book in the series, which should be especially useful for the classroom as well as to our understanding of the role of non-state actors in the development arena. We wholeheartedly recommend it and, as always, welcome comments from our readers.

Thomas G. Weiss, The CUNY Graduate Center, New York, USA
Rorden Wilkinson, University of Manchester, UK
June 2013

Notes

1 Thomas G. Weiss and Rorden Wilkinson, eds, *International Organization and Global Governance* (London: Routledge, 2013); and Thomas G. Weiss and Rorden Wilkinson, "Rethinking Global Governance: Complexity, Authority, Power, Change," *International Studies Quarterly* 58, no. 2 (2014).

2 Ian Bache and Matthew Flinders, eds, *Multi-level Governance* (Oxford: Oxford University Press, 2004).

3 Union of International Associations, *Yearbook of International Organizations, edition 48, volume 5* (Brussels, Belgium: Union of International Associations, 2011).

4 James N. Rosenau, "Toward an Ontology for Global Governance," in *Approaches to Global Governance Theory*, ed. Martin Hewson and Timothy J. Sinclair (Albany, NY: State University of New York, 1999), 293.

5 Peter J. Willetts, *Non-Governmental Organizations in World Politics* (London: Routledge, 2011).

6 Roy J. Hauya and Jonathan M. Makuwira, *Basic Education in Malawi: Objectives, Problems and Perspectives* (Blantyre, Malawi: Dzuka Publishing, 1996).

7 See, for example, "Civil Society Organizations (CSOs) and the Changing Nature of African Politics: The Case of the CSO–Government Relationship in Malawi," *Journal of Asian and African Studies* 46, no. 6 (2011): 615–28; and "The Role of Civil Society in Peacebuilding in Fragile Democracies: The Case of Malawi," *Global Development Studies* 4 (2006): 250–67.

Acknowledgments

The first half of 2011 was the beginning of a journey which has resulted in this book. The desire to embark on this project was inspired by a number of people too numerous to mention. My casual conversation with prolific academic writers such as Professor Joseph Siracusa, Associate Professor Paul Battersby, Associate Professor Tahmina Rashid and Professor Jock McCulloch was immensely inspirational. Thanks to Professor Siracusa for his support for linking me with Regina Books which was supposed to publish this book. It was unfortunate that they closed their offices just when I was about to submit the manuscript.

I sincerely acknowledge the support from the Royal Melbourne Institute of Technology (RMIT) University and, indeed, Associate Professor Paul Battersby for approving my research leave which enabled me to focus on researching and writing the book in Malawi. My sincere appreciation goes to Associate Professor Daimon Kambewa of Bunda College of Agriculture, for his support in hosting me in his Extension Department. To Dr Stanley Khaila, Dr David Mkwambisi and Dr Charles Masangano, I register my appreciation. To the many non-governmental organizations with which I interacted in Malawi, I owe my appreciation.

Thanks to Mr Kent Kafatiya for accommodating me at his lodge during my sabbatical.

There is nothing more devastating than to be told "the publisher is no more." This was the case when I was about to submit my manuscript to Regina. In my desperation to identify a new publisher, I bumped into a selfless colleague, Dr Aiden Warren, who suggested I contact Nicola Parkin at Routledge. This was it! Mate, thanks indeed.

Working with Professor Thomas Weiss and Professor Rorden Wilkinson, the series editors, was immensely educative and rewarding. Their guidance in the process leading to the production of this book was invaluable. Thanks to Nicola Parkin for everything.

The task of accomplishing an academic piece of writing like this can be emotionally draining. Such was the case. I want to thank my wife Mercy for putting up with missing me at a time when she needed me most. Her encouragement and selfless support is what kept me going. To my daughters Patience and Mphatso, you did not miss in vain. I never stopped thinking about sons Dalitso, and Mayesero as well as daughter Dorophy all of which were the atoms and fuel to this work.

Abbreviations

ABNGO	Association of Brazilian NGOs
ACFID	Australian Council for International Development
ANCP	Australia NGO Cooperation Program
AusAID	Australian Agency for International Development
BBC	British Broadcasting Corporation
CAFOD	Catholic Agency for Overseas Development
CBO	community-based organization
CCAP	Church of Central Africa, Presbyterian
CODE-NGO	Caucus of Development NGO Networks
COMESA	Common Market for Eastern and Southern Africa
CONGOMA	Council for NGOs in Malawi
CSO	civil society organization
DAC	Development Assistance Committee
DANIDA	Danish International Development Agency
DfID	UK Department for International Development
DONGO	donor-driven/organized NGOs
DPP	Democratic Progressive Party
ECED	Early Childhood Education and Development
GNI	gross national income
HAP	Humanitarian Accountability Project
HHCDO	Homa Hills Community Development Organization
IDEP	Institute of Economic Development and Planning
IGO	intergovernmental organization
INGO	international NGO
IWDA	International Women's Development Agency
JICA	Japan International Cooperation Agency
LNWDA	Leitana Nehan Women's Development Agency
MDGs	Millennium Development Goals
MELF	Monitoring, Evaluation and Learning Framework
MFI	micro-finance institution

MoU	memorandum of understanding
NGDO	nongovernmental development organization
NGO	nongovernmental organization
NNGO	Northern NGOs
OD	organizational development
ODA	overseas development assistance
OECD	Organisation for Economic Co-operation and Development
PAMFORM	Participatory Methodologies Form of Kenya
PM&E	participatory monitoring and evaluation
SIDA	Swedish International Development Agency
SNGO	Southern NGOs
TNGO	transitional NGO
UN	United Nations
UNEP	United Nations Environment Programme
UNICEF	United Nations Children's Education Fund
USAID	United States Agency for International Development
VANI	Voluntary Agencies Network in India
WASH	Water, Sanitation and Hygiene
WTO	World Trade Organization

Introduction

- **Defining NGDOs**
- **Core values, beliefs and roles espoused by NGDOs**
- **The roadmap**

The role nongovernmental development organizations (NGDOs) play in development has become an area of intense debate. Just over a decade ago one of the leading scholars, theorists and practitioners in the field of development, Alan Fowler, remarked: "The tasks NGDOs set for themselves, and the expectations of those that finance them, are complex and (probably too) demanding."[1] Over the years, this statement has been affirmed by the sheer number of books, articles and commentaries on the role of the NGDO sector in poverty reduction. The demand comes amid increasing failure of states to provide their citizenry with the needed basic social services that alleviate poverty. As such, NGDOs have been drawn into filling this void.

On 25 February 2004, the BBC News ran an "African Live Debate" on the topic "NGOs: Achievers or Deceivers?"[2] in which the nongovernmental organization (NGO) sector was under scrutiny. The topic was confined to NGO work in Africa. Two questions guided the debate: Are NGOs a force for good in Africa or are they failing in their promises? How democratic and accountable are NGOs? Some of the responses that emerged from the debate are of great significance to the theme of this book. A few of these comments are examined in light of what has now become a very complex and polarized topic in development discourse.

Box I.1 Comments on NGOs from the BBC debate

Ideally, NGOs are expected to help Africans overcome many ills in the continent. But, unfortunately, in a poverty-stricken continent, where accountability counts less, ninety percent of NGOs in Africa are corrupt business outfits. They deceive their Western donors and contribute nothing to the society.

True, many NGO's in Africa are not established in the best interests of the targets they claim to serve. Only a few are genuine, and even so, they are spread thinly everywhere and make no impact at all. Many are money minting factories by their directors, others serve the interests of their sponsors abroad. It's high time NGOs that are fuelling poverty were wound up!

Some NGOs are doing a wonderful job. In Bayelsa State of Nigeria, UNICEF virtually runs the Primary Health Care system. The Government cannot even provide Immunization twice a year. So NGOs keep up the good work!

NGOs are another way for western citizens to avoid paying tax while enriching themselves.

NGOs are crucial for delivery of social services where the state is unwilling or unable to do so. However, their role is to supplement the government not to replace it. Anything else is simply unsustainable.

It is hard to generalize about the performance and integrity of the numerous NGOs operating across Africa. What may be true of one NGO, may not necessarily be true of another. My advice is for us to refrain from a blanket indictment or adulation of "all" NGOs. Such an approach obscures the reality of NGO involvement in Africa's development. Also, whatever, we say, however, let us not suggest that our governments should take over from the NGOs. We are too incompetent for that. Aren't the NGOs in Africa because we couldn't do it ourselves?

Source: (news.bbc.co.uk/2/hi/africa/3502733.stm)

The varied comments on the debate highlight not only the complexity of the development terrain but also the changing donor dynamics and the culture of the NGDO sector. Furthermore, these comments invite a critical reflection on their claims and counterclaims within the development industry. Considering an array of competing agendas by the international aid agencies, the speed of globalization, and the desire for change by the people who are affected by poverty, the debate about the role of the NGDO sector in contributing to poverty reduction continues to unfold with different shape, tone and intensity. One thing is certain, NGDOs are here to stay. Not only does the ever-increasing desire to Make Poverty History legitimize NGDOs' presence but it also offers a glimmer of hope as the world continues to strive to deal with development challenges both in the developing and developed world.

While the developing world holds onto hope for a better tomorrow insofar as development is concerned, the changing social, economic, political and environmental landscape does not seem friendly at all. As service providers, NGDOs are constantly confronted with multiple realities which dictate the way they do things. The question is, how quickly do they adapt to the changing realities of life? While the answer to such a broad question may remain elusive, there is no shortage of goodwill among NGDOs which, in their quest to foster social change, encounter many challenges along the way. The academy, meanwhile, continues to produce thousands of graduates of international development or development studies who make their way into the real world with conflicting messages of what development is all about. Furthermore, the nature of the development studies curriculum has not fully come under the radar of serious scrutiny. Yet today, the NGDO sector is infiltrated by graduates who claim expertise in development but are oblivious of the changing nature of the development landscape.

Nongovernmental Development Organizations and the Poverty Reduction Agenda: The Moral Crusaders offers a new direction and thinking about the NGDO sector. Its primary audience is students of international development or any other sector of social development who are interested in engaging in new thinking in the way we theorize development and its praxis. While other books[3] have offered a comprehensive debate on NGOs, this book takes a step further. First, it contextualizes NGDOs within the popular development discourse by challenging the orthodoxy seemingly entrenched in the minds of many in the development field, academia and research institutions. Second, the book redefines critical development discourses such as aid, partnerships, capacity development, leadership and learning and, using case studies, draws lessons that may help us understand the tensions and contradictions in the discourses, thereby alerting us to the way we reconceptualize development in the modern era. The aim is to highlight the gaps left by other contributors to the debates. In highlighting these, I aim to point out that NGDOs as conduits between the international aid agencies and their beneficiaries have an opportunity to make a difference by "coming down to earth" or risk being conduits that no longer command an identity of being the conscience of the world,[4] but are merely propagators of the neoliberal agenda of the Washington consensus. At the same time, while a lot of attention has been given to understanding international NGDOs like World Vision International, Oxfam, Care

International, Plan International, to name just a few, this book offers a critical analysis of grassroots organizations—those NGDOs founded and established by locals and operating at the deepest end of the development context.

To date, the debate on the role of nongovernmental organizations in development has been paradoxical largely because of the "non" in its nomenclature: the reality on the ground seems contrary. It is therefore the focus of this book to canvas in great detail the role of NGOs in development, with a particular focus on how development is understood and operationalized by emerging local NGOs and their networks. The moral crusade, as a theme of this book, permeates every single chapter in the book by teasing out the drive in each of the concepts presented. It is, however, not an easy task. As Lewis and Kanji[5] rightly point out, the increasing mushrooming of the NGOs in the twenty-first century is a challenging phenomenon because they are not a singular entity that can easily be generalized. What makes the study of NGDOs even more difficult is their differing roles, aspirations, motivation, philosophies, values, organizational structures and funding mechanisms. Of late the NGDO sector has been drawn into the task of responding to the popular Millennium Development Goals (MDGs) which, by their nature, appeal to the international chorus on ending extreme poverty. However, based on the dynamics and the environment within which they operate, one thing is clear: NGDOs have an immense task to contribute to these goals. The consolation, however, lies in the current thinking by development scholars, practitioners and advocates who purport to represent those on the fringes of society—those whose lives today lie in the dark and fading shadows of hope for tomorrow. It is the desire of this book to analyze various alternatives for NGDO effectiveness in the field of international development.

Defining NGDOs

Defining NGDOs is by no means easy. Establishing clarity of what is meant by nongovernmental development organizations (NGDOs) is highly useful. Definitions, while they provide clarity, can at times be deceiving if we stick to truism. However, we do sometimes need to gain a fair amount of understanding of concepts and ideas in order to make linkages between issues. The term NGDO was first coined by Alan Fowler in his classic book *Striking a Balance*,[6] in which his focus was a critical reflection of a particular type of NGO—those involved in development. In order to understand NGDOs, it is important to step back and canvas the meaning of the root of the term nongovernmental organization.

There are various discussions in the literature about the terminology "NGOs."[7] Interestingly, the discussion has a broad focus on non-government organizations. There are two obvious problems with this sort of analysis. Although the term "*non-government*" is seen as a negative way to describe an organization, suggestions for other terminologies have not engendered any enduring alternatives. Also, the number of organizations that fit under the term NGO is seen to be varied as well as wide. This diversity potentially renders the term NGO meaningless. Yet, despite the criticism, the term remains enduring and is applied to essentially mean *organizations that work for the aid and development of others, without direct profit for themselves.* The most popular definitions of NGOs tend to describe particular characteristics in common: independence, non-profit, voluntary, and not for the immediate benefit of those who are members. Based on this kind of definition, NGOs can constitute on array of actors based on or fitting two if not three frameworks—that is, those known to be non-profit, voluntary or pursuing charity. These labels deceivingly sound different but, in general, they mean the same thing. The only difference is where the labels are commonly applied, and more importantly, their historical origin. Najam, Lewis and Kanji, and Ronalds have provided a comprehensive overview of terms that elucidate the diversity of NGDOs.[8] In this book, I highlight a few as a matter of clarifying some misconceptions of their meanings.

Box I.2 Diversity of NGOs

- INGO: implies an organization that works in several countries but maintains its headquarters in a developed country.
- NNGO: Northern NGO, that is, an NGO based in a developed or industrialized country.
- SNGO: Southern NGO, that is, an NGO based in a developing country.
- TNGO: Transitional NGO—an NGO with a very multi-national structure, running programs in many countries, and also with global or supranational governance or management.
- CBOs: community-based organizations—this is a more grass-roots membership or non-membership organization.
- DONGOs: donor-oriented/organized NGOs.
- QUANGOs: quasi-NGOs—normally those NGOs established by government-run NGOs (GRINGOs). These can also be known as government-owned NGOs (GONGOs).

  Source: (David Lewis and Nazneen Kanji, *Non-Governmental Organisations and Development* (London: Routledge, 2009): 9–10)

The "Northern" and "Southern" discourses here need to be understood within a wider context of colonial and post-colonial debate. These notions are power-laden and convey meanings of "superiority" (Northern) and "inferiority" (Southern). This is more like other binaries such as developed/developing, rich/poor. In view of these nomenclatures, it is highly important that we carefully understand these within a wider context of discourse as power.[9]

One popular concept that is defined in tandem with the NGO is the idea of civil society. As Ronalds[10] clarifies, the concept is broadly used to denote those parts of society that are neither directly controlled by state nor form part of society's commercial activity (market). Based on this, it can be understood to imply that all NGOs, irrespective of their activity and focus, are part of civil society. This fluidity is a matter of concern, especially when development NGOs are defined as organizations that are essentially conduits of donor agencies or those that are concerned with promotion of social, economic and political change in society. This, in a broader sense, could be termed development. However, when one considers the complexity of the motion of development, it is rather hard to exclude NGOs that are advocacy-oriented as non-development organizations. Hence improving the quality of life implies dealing with the complex tapestry of social, economic, political, environmental and cultural elements which, when viewed from a holistic angle, offers insightful reconceptualization of what a development NGO is. For example, it is often perceived that civil society organizations such as trade unions are not development organizations, yet in their advocacy work they significantly contribute to the public good and quality of life. A more nuanced definition of civil society, in this case, needs revisiting in light of the changing nature of not only NGOs but civil society. This will be dealt with later in the next chapter, but in canvassing the various meanings of the concept of NGO, we also need to understand another concept closely associated with civil society: the *third sector*.

While it is equally problematic to define the third sector clearly, one consolation is that the concept helps to clarify the roles development NGOs have in enhancing human well-being.[11] In this case the third sector is understood to mean a world of institutions that neither fit into the government nor the business sectors. The third sector therefore is premised on fundamental principles of voluntarism but at the same time tapping into both the business and government principles to advance the agenda of contributing to social, economic and political well-being. Consequently, third sector institutions are fundamentally:

- formal—institutionalized;
- private—non-government;
- non-profit-distributing—no ownership of profit accruing from any undertaking of the organization; and
- self-governing—managing its own affairs.

Inherent in this framework is the role of the third sector. Essentially, it can be deduced that the third sector plays a crucial role in strengthening the role of both the government (state) and business sectors. Translated differently, NGOs concerned with development are controlled by two major development forces—the exogenous and endogenous development paradigms. The interplay among the three (exogenous, endogenous and third sector) cannot be overemphasized. The third sector, therefore, is a space which, according to Burkett and Bedi,[12] plays a vital role in:

- enhancing organic participatory development;
- facilitating access to locally available resources and enhancing bottom-up approaches to development;
- minimizing the mentality of a one-size-fits-all development approach;

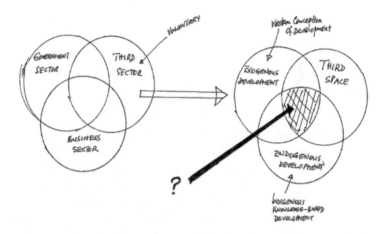

Figure I.1 Third sector, Western conception of development and indigenous knowledge (Adapted from Ingrid Burkett and Harvinder Bedi, *What in the World...? Global Lessons, Inspirations and Experiences in Community Development*, January 2007, www.iacdglobal.org/files/WITWReport08012007.pdf)

- linking local development initiatives into the global context and vice-versa;
- enhancing local voices being heard;
- enhancing local development ownership; and
- facilitating acceptance of difference and respect for local cultures and knowledge within the development context.

Core values, beliefs and roles espoused by NGDOs

This book is about NGDOs' moral crusade against poverty in all its forms of manifestation. Understanding the role of NGDOs requires us to appreciate fully what motivates and drives them into action. At the heart of NGDO operations are values and beliefs. Values are principles that NGDOs commit to uphold in all aspects of their work. It is these values that further dictate the nature and quality of relationships they establish with their counterparts, beneficiaries, donor agencies and government. Values also play a pivotal role in how NGDOs conduct their internal affairs or organizational management. So, what are values and beliefs and why do they matter in development NGOs? In a nutshell, values and beliefs are expressions of what an organization stands for. Values and beliefs define an organization's identity. For example, these values and beliefs may be driven by the desire for social justice. This ideological platform is translated into practice by such actions as engaging in the campaign "Make Poverty History"; or through the provision of basic social services to all in need regardless of race, color, class; promotion of the rights of marginalized and vulnerable people in society; support for active participation and empowerment of women and less privileged people. NGDO values, beliefs, missions and visions are its compass. Chung Kwak wrote:

> If the NGO movement is not to suffer a loss of credibility, we must all affirm, uphold, and practice certain core values ... They include the values of unselfishness, the value of a life lived for the well-being of others, such as the parent who sacrifices for his or her children or the patriot who serves the nation ... If we degenerate into special interest groups that have self-centered, narrow purposes, we are nothing more than one more competing voice seeking attention and resources. Let us live for the sake of others.[13]

The significance of this claim is seen in both theory and practice. Over the years the NGO sector has made some strides in articulating its desire to fulfill this self-imposed responsibility. For example, the

Toronto Declaration of NGO Core Values[14] is perhaps one of the most comprehensive summaries of what drives NGDOs to undertake what the theme of this book is all about: a moral crusade against poverty.

Box I.3 NGO fundamental values and beliefs

Toronto Declaration of NGO Core Values

I Service beyond self

NGOs, on the whole, are founded to serve others. While responsibly maintaining itself, an NGO integrates self-development and individual concerns with public concerns, focusing on higher, broader, and more public levels of service. An NGO should conduct its activities for the sake of others, whether the public at large or a particular segment of the public. NGO practitioners are to be exemplars of genuine giving out of concern for the welfare of others without the primary goal of their own enhancement or profit.

II Respect for human rights

An NGO should not violate any person's fundamental human rights, with which each person is endowed, as recognized for example in the Universal Declaration of Human Rights. An NGO should recognize that all people are born free and equal in dignity and rights (Article 1), and should be sensitive to the moral values, religion, customs, traditions, and cultures of the communities they serve. Recognizing that the family is a fundamental natural group unit of society promoting human rights and human dignity (Article 16), an NGO should respect the integrity of families. An NGO should respect each individual's right of freedom of thought, conscience, and religion (Article 18).

III Maintain a vision

NGO practitioners should be visionaries, not only seeing the reality of the world as it is, but also envisioning the world as it should be. NGOs should maintain their founding spirit and passion, keeping their tangible dreams while learning from their victories and failures.

IV Responsibility

NGOs, entrusted with a responsibility to the public, should take ownership of the task at hand, taking the initiative and proactively pulling together resources of all types in order to find and implement feasible solutions. NGO practitioners are to demonstrate ownership of their NGO, be accountable for the execution and outcomes of their NGO's stated and expected goals, and strive for excellence in their work.

V Cooperation beyond borders

NGOs have a shared responsibility to address the serious challenges confronting humanity. Significant progress toward world peace and global well-being can be fostered through inter-religious, intercultural, and interracial work, and across artificial barriers of politics, race, and ethnicity that tend to separate people and their institutions. NGOs should maintain ethical, cooperative relationships with other NGOs, and should partner where possible and appropriate for the sake of the greater public good. An NGO should be willing to work beyond these borders, within the limits of its organizing documents and with organizations and individuals that share common values and objectives.

VI Public mindedness

An NGO should have a spirit of public mindedness. Public money must not be misused for selfish purposes and all public assets are to be treated with utmost seriousness, as a sacred public trust. An NGO should exhibit a responsible and caring attitude toward the environment in all of its activities. An NGO should recognize that its conduct and activities impact on the public's perception of NGOs and that it shares responsibility for the public's trust of NGOs.

VII Accountability

An NGO should be accountable for its actions and decisions, primarily to the community it serves, and also to its funding agencies, the government, staff and volunteers, members, partner organizations, and the public at large.

VIII Truthfulness

An NGO should be truthful in its dealings with its donors, project beneficiaries, staff, members, partner organizations, government, and the general public. Any information given out should be accurate, whether regarding itself and its projects, or regarding any individual, organization, project, or legislation it opposes or is discussing. An NGO must be strongly opposed to, and not a willing partner to, corruption, bribery, and other financial improprieties or illegalities.

IX Transparency

An NGO should be transparent in its dealings with the government, the public, donors, partners, beneficiaries, and other interested parties, except for personal matters and proprietary information. Except as needed to protect human rights, an NGO's basic financial information, governance structure, activities, and listing of officers and partnerships shall be open and accessible to public scrutiny and the NGO is to make effort to inform the public about its work and the origin and use of its resources.

X Nonprofit integrity

To maintain its integrity as an NGO, the organization is to be organized and operated as a not-for-profit organization, with any surplus generated through its operations to be utilized solely to help the organization fulfill its mission and objectives. The organization is not to be operated for the primary purpose of carrying on a trade or business, unrelated to the mission and stated objectives.

XI Comprehensive viewpoint

An NGO should seek to understand, without prejudice, the needs and circumstances of all sides in any conflict situation.

XII Voluntarism

Rather than required to exist by law, NGOs are formed by private initiative, resulting from the voluntary actions of individuals who have chosen to pursue a shared interest of concern. The

retaining of voluntary values and principles shall remain a primary
force in the way of working of the NGO.

Source: (World Congress of NGOs, 2007,
www.wango.org/congress2007/declaration.aspx)

As value-based organizations, NGDO conduct (in light of these values)
has sparked a heated debate. While values are considered essential to
what NGDOs represent in their quest for social justice, contradictions
and tensions between theory and practice remain.[15] As their roles and
responsibilities change, NGDOs find themselves under constant criticism,
for example, in using their privileged positions, power and resources to
influence and shape the values of others, especially those that they purport
to support. Whether these values can be expressed through service
delivery or advocacy is also an issue of intense debate. Lately, the practice of NGDOs or civil society as a watch dog[16] or the conscience of
the world,[17] has taken a twist amid mounting revelations and scrutiny
of how NGDOs are, in actual fact, accountable, transparent and consistent in living up to their claims of comparative advantage[18] and
being proactive as a rapid response in times of humanitarian action.
With limited empirical evidence of their effectiveness, the NGDO debate
on the core values and beliefs is extremely polarized. Some commentators hold their optimism, seeing NGOs as heading in the right
direction as long as they change their *modus operandi*.[19] Other commentators[20] remain cautious and see these actors as propagators of a
new policy agenda which is in sharp contradiction to indigenous
knowledge systems. Therefore, while the core values and beliefs sound
rosy, how NGDOs translate them to their daily practices is critical.
Even where the values provide legitimacy, the bone of contention
remains that unless there is evidence of positive change in the lives of
the people, those values will continue to be under constant scrutiny.[21]

The roadmap

In *Nongovernmental Development Organizations and the Poverty Reduction
Agenda: The Moral Crusaders*, I navigate the debates through six main
chapters. Following a concise introduction in this section, Chapter 1
contains two major parts. The first part locates NGDOs in historical context by highlighting that NGDOs are not here by default but have appeared
at the center stage of the development landscape through an historical
metamorphosis. The idea of civil society, in particular, as a cursory
event to the emergence of the NGDOs/NGOs is very important. The

chapter thus provides a detailed account of the origin and growth of NGDOs since the mid-1850s through the post-war era. The chapter elucidates the following key areas: the origin of NGDOs (the focus here will be international NGOs, or INGOs); the ideological position that influenced their growth; the NGDO sector during the world wars; post-war expansion and the shifting ideological position; structural changes in the operations of NGDO historical development; and NGDOs' influence on global and local politics.

The second part of Chapter 1 discusses the linkage between NGDOs and foreign development assistance (aid), arguing that NGDOs' involvement in the aid industry has both historical and political influence. At the center of this is the moral drive behind aid giving and its use to reduce poverty. The chapter covers issues such as: the history of overseas development assistance (ODA); NGO involvement in development or service provision in the post-war era; NGDO-donor cooperation and its implications for development; aid conditionalities and its impact on development; the Paris Declaration; and donor-driven development programs, including tensions and contradictions on development, aid effectiveness and efficiency.

Chapter 2 critically analyzes the discourse of "partnerships" and the motives behind such relationships in the development sector. The chapter specifically covers the following key issues: competing views and meanings of partnerships; NGDO partnerships with states; NGDO partnerships with Northern NGDOs; NGDO partnerships with other NGDOs; NGDO partnerships with their beneficiaries; case analysis of partnerships; and challenges and opportunities in partnerships.

Directly linked to the notion of partnerships is *capacity development*, which Chapter 3 analyzes in great length. In light of the tensions and contradictions, NGO capacity to deliver services has come under the spotlight. This chapter examines the debate within the context of competing power dynamics and highlights that building NGDO capacity is one thing, but doing so in the context of power dynamics is another.

In Chapter 4, the debate gravitates around issues of NGDO accountability. The chapter offers insightful accounts of some of the challenges NGDOs encounter in ensuring accountability not only to self but also to both their donors and primary constituencies. NGO leadership and management have become critical to the success of development programs. Chapter 5 discusses some of these issues through NGDO case studies, while Chapter 6 offers some insights into how NGDOs can become learning organizations and agents of change through a process of reflection on their own work and experiences.

The book draws together some key issues in Chapter 7, documents lessons learned and suggests some ideas on how NGDOs can improve and contribute to development and poverty reduction.

This book does not, by any means, intend to provide a comprehensive account of these critical development discourses as solutions to the challenges of development. Rather the book is intended to ignite more reflection not only in the NGDO sector but all those concerned with the plight of the poor. The nongovernmental development organizations, as a part of broader civil society, are value-laden organizations. Their contribution to the development field is quite diverse. Although the past decade has seen a significant shift in the roles of the sector from mainstream service delivery to advocacy, there are apparent contradictions in how NGDOs translate their definitions into action. The environment within which NGDOs operate is very complex because it is imbued in the social, economic, political, cultural and environmental contexts which, in themselves, are complex. Constant negotiations and repositioning of their development agendas seem inevitable. Given that development is political, NGDOs have to confront multiple realities by constantly negotiating with multiple stakeholders. This book aims to bring some of the complexity of this debate to the fore. However, before going deeper into the debate, Chapter 1 charts the history and the morality of giving, which over the years has mutated into foreign development assistance.

Notes

1 Alan Fowler, *Partnerships: Negotiating Relationships: A Resource for Non-Governmental Development Organisations*, INTRAC Occasional Papers No. 32 (Oxford: INTRAC, 2000), vii.
2 BBC, "NGOs: Achievers or Deceivers?" news.bbc.co.uk/2/hi/africa/3502733. stm.
3 See for example David Lewis and Nazneen Kanji, *Non-Governmental Organisations and Development* (London: Routledge, 2009); Paul Ronalds, *The Change Imperative: Creating the Next Generation NGO* (Sterling, Va.: Kumarian Press, 2010).
4 Peter Willetts, *The Conscience of the World: The Influence of Non-Governmental Organisations in the UN System* (Washington, DC: The Brookings Institution, 1996).
5 Lewis and Kanji, *Non-Governmental Organisations and Development*.
6 Alan Fowler, *Striking a Balance: A Guide to Enhancing the Effectiveness of Non-Governmental Organisations in International Development* (London: Earthscan, 1997).
7 David C. Korten, *Getting to the 21st Century: Voluntary Action and the Global Agenda* (West Hartford, Conn.: Kumarian Press, 1990); Michael Edwards and David Hulme, "NGOs and Development: Performance and

Accountability in the New World Order," Background Paper for the International Workshop on *NGOs and Development: Performance and Accountability in the New World Order*, University of Manchester, 27–29 June 1994; Collin Ball and Leith L. Dunn, *Non-Government Organisations: Guidelines for Good Policy and Practice* (London: The Commonwealth Foundation, 1996), 18–20; Stephen Commins, "NGOs: Ladles in the Global Soup Kitchen," *Development in Practice* 9, no. 5 (November 1999): 619–22.

8 Adil Najam, "NGO Accountability: A Conceptual Framework," *Development Policy Review* 14, no. 4 (1996): 39–353; Lewis and Kanji, *Non-Governmental Organisations and Development*; Ronalds, *The Change Imperative*.

9 Michel Foucault, *Power/Knowledge* (Brighton: Harvester, 1980).

10 Ronalds, *The Change Imperative*, 3.

11 Helmut K. Anheier and Wolfgang Seibel, ed., *The Third Sector: Comparative Studies of Non-profit Organizations* (New York: de Gruyter, 1990); M.G. Deepika and Amalendu Jyotishi, "The Role of Third Sector in Development of Drought Prone Regions: Insights from Kachchh, Gujarat," *International NGO Journal* 6, no. 8 (2011): 181–92.

12 Ingrid Burkett and Harvinder Bedi, *What in the World … ? Global Lessons, Inspirations and Experiences in Community Development*; January 2007, www.iacdglobal.org/files/WITWReport08012007.pdf.

13 Chung H. Kwak, "NGOs Core Values and True Responsibility," in *Culture of Responsibility and the Role of NGOs*, ed. Taj I. Hamad, Frederick A. Swarts and Anne R. Smart (St Paul, Minn.: Pragon House, 2003), 13.

14 World Congress of NGOs (WANGO), *Toronto Declaration of NGO Core Values*, 2007, www.wango.org/congress2007/declaration.aspx.

15 Tina Wallace, "Institutionalising Gender in UK NGOs," *Development in Practice* 8, no. 2 (1998): 159–71; Sarah Mukasa "Are Expatriate Staff Necessary in International Development NGOs? A Case Study of an International NGO in Uganda," *CVO International Working Paper 4* (1999), eprints.lse.ac.uk/29092/1/int-work-paper4.pdf; Jonathan J. Makuwira, "Non-Governmental Organizations (NGOs) and Participatory Development in Basic Education in Malawi," *Current Issues in Comparative Education* 6, no. 2, (2004), www.tc.columbia.edu/cice/articles/jm162.htm.

16 Dorothea Baur and Peter H. Schmitz, "Corporations and NGOs: When Accountability Leads to Co-optation," *Journal of Business Ethics* 106, no. 1 (March 2011): 9–21.

17 Willetts, *The Conscience of the World*.

18 Terje Tvedt, *Angels of Mercy or Development Diplomats? NGOs and Foreign Aid* (Trenton, N.J.: African World Press, 1998).

19 Ronalds, *The Change Imperative*; Derek Fee, *How to Manage an Aid Exit Strategy: The Future of Development Aid* (London: Zed Books, 2012).

20 Nicola Banks and David Hulme, "The Role of NGOs and Civil Society in Development and Poverty Reduction," *Brooks World Poverty Institute Working Paper 171* (2012), www.bwpi.manchester.ac.uk/resources/Working-Papers/bwpi-wp-17112.pdf.

21 Ann Neville, "Values and Legitimacy of Third Sector Service Delivery Organisations: Evidence from Australia," *Voluntas* 20, no. 1 (2009): 71–89.

1   NGDO history and aid modalities

- **The history**
- **Understanding today's NGDO world**
- **NGDOs as organizations in the development context**
- **NGDOs in the development environment**
- **NGDOs and aid modalities**
- **A brief history of aid**
- **The aid debate outside NGDOs**
- **NGDOs and aid conditionality**
- **Conclusion**

NGDOs have evolved over a long period of time. While in some instances it can be claimed that their formation is a relatively recent phenomenon within the political economy of modern Western states, these actors, their values, and institutions that drive their agenda in relief, rehabilitation and development, have a long and neglected history.[1] This chapter aims to survey the history of the NGDO sector by selectively analyzing its origin, ideological position that influences its growth, the post-war expansion and the shifting ideological agenda, structural changes in its operations, and the influence on the social, political and economic sphere of life in the modern era. The perspectives raised in this chapter will mostly be those of international NGOs, development NGOs, and broader philanthropic organizations. The second section of the chapter explores aid modalities by specifically analyzing the role of aid in development. The focus is how NGDOs, as conduits of donor agencies, use aid in their development projects.

The NGDO sector's presence on the global stage is driven by a number of factors. This continued support for the public generosity of philanthropists is largely driven by spiritual and moral imperatives. It is from this position that historians are very keen to delve deep into understanding what really drives this spirit of benevolent behavior.

It is now estimated that up to 70 percent of the population of the Western countries make regular charitable donations.[2] Of this population, roughly 25 percent also volunteer their time to offer service to those believed to be in need. This is, by definition, philanthropy,[3] and is premised on the platform of offering service in order to advance the general quality and well-being of humans, especially the marginalized and disenfranchised—those living on the fringes of society. In a nutshell, the philanthropic or NGDO sector's metamorphosis has largely been driven by the desire for social justice.

The history

The status of the nongovernmental development sector has evolved over a period of time. The diversity and reach of these organizations is difficult to quantify. According to *The Global Journal*[4] the entry and usage of the term "nongovernmental organizations" on the United Nations (UN) Charter at the end of World War II had a lot of influence over what was to come. However, the onset of the modern era NGOs has been preceded by religious orders, missionary groups, and scientific societies which engaged in cross-cutting issues of socio-political significance of the time. Many of the organizations included both secular and religious institutions. For example, the Roman Catholic monastic order still exists now. The evolution of the early NGOs was mostly significant in such areas as political activism, humanitarianism, and social justice. A few of these include but are not limited to:

- Society for the Recovery of the Drowned, in 1767;
- A Universal Confederation of the Friends of Truth, in 1790;
- The Royal Jennerian Society, in 1803, to fight smallpox;
- The Pennsylvania Society for the Relief of Free Negros Unlawfully Held in Bondage, in 1775;
- British and Foreign Anti-Slavery Society, in 1839;
- World Alliance of Young Men's Christian Associations, in 1855; and
- Red Cross Movement, in 1863, for neutral assistance to the wounded in conflict.[5]

In his paper *The Rise and Fall of Transnational Civil Society: The Evolution of International Non-Governmental Organizations since 1839*, Thomas Davies[6] observes that while by 1854 only six INGOs had been founded, by the turn of the century the number increased to 163, and by 1945 over 1,000 INGOs had been established.[7] By 2007, it is estimated that well over 60,000 INGOs were established around the world.[8]

As earlier stated, while the increase in the number of INGOs has been the hallmark of the debate, the sector's contribution to the current state of international development discourse has its own evolutionary and historical trajectory. The INGOs and other transnational civil society are said to have played a significant role in bringing the Cold War to an end; contributed towards the redefinition of development and security to include humanitarian concerns; and facilitated the institutionalization of international agreements such as the 1987 Montreal Protocol and the 1997 Ottawa Landmines Convention.[9]

On the political front, NGOs have evolved with strong influence on activism. Most notably the anti-slavery movement, the founding of the League of Nations and United Nations organizations have had a lot of influence on the role that the sector plays in reducing poverty today. However, while the growth of the sector in all these endeavors is noteworthy, it is also important to note that the growth came in waves of increased and decreased need. For example, the pre- and post-world war era; the Great Depression and other eventful occurrences saw the number of NGOs swell and dwindle. Also, global demographic changes had a great influence in shaping the role of the current NGDO sector. Take, for example, urbanization, democratization, globalization, interstate peace building, transnational political issues and other related issues—all these have shaped the way the current NGOs operate. The birth of such INGOs as Oxfam, World Vision International, Plan International, to name a few, mirror such a trajectory where altruism, faith and mere philanthropy coalesce to shape the order in which human morality is dispensed. The section that follows highlights some of the current trends in this history.

Understanding today's NGDO world

The overview in the preceding section has provided ample evidence that the current role of NGDOs has a long history. However, over the years the changing nature of the sector has prompted development theorists to examine NGDOs and contextualized their role in different frameworks. A plethora of literature[10] includes many different frameworks or approaches to understand NGDOs. These include theories from political science, economic theory and social-origin theory. Each of these theories offers a unique perspective in elucidating the role nongovernmental development organizations play in various sectors of social life. In particular, these theories offer multiple, and sometimes competing accountabilities operating within the

NGDO sector and, also, different points of legitimacy to their roles and work.

Political Science Theory likens NGDOs to political parties, arguing that both NGDO and political parties are organizationally separate from the state and market and both are also accountable to a limited constituency. Despite this feature, there is also recognition that NGDOs and political parties serve the desires and needs of a much broader group in society. However, in both cases, there is a tension between means and ends. For NGDOs, this tension is between achieving the ideals of change for the good and sustaining their own survival as organizations.

State Theory, according to Salamon and Anheier,[11] understands NGDOs as operating in mediation between the state apparatus and communities. This theory sees interactive mutuality between the NGDO sector and the state. This argument is actually premised on the belief that the NGDO sector can be effective and instrumental if it works collaboratively with the state in the delivery and mediation of social services as well as the provision of resources. However, while the theory sounds strong, the weakness is seen in the NGDOs' funding base. In this regard, the donor wields too much power which often sways NGDO focus from its constituency—the target beneficiaries—and creates difficulties in incentives for efficiency.

Another theory is from an *anthropological perspective*, which understands NGDOs as complex social systems in themselves. The central issue is how their operations and interactions contribute to sense making in a dynamic and complex world beyond the organization.[12]

The Social-Origin Theory, on the other hand, looks at NGDOs as embedded in society, serving various constituencies.[13] Their work can therefore be understood in terms of the different representations and participation of different stakeholders. While all these theories add to our understanding of NGDOs, especially in terms of their accountabilities and responsibilities, the more general approach has been to understand them as organizations. On the one hand, there seems to be an attempt to understand NGDOs by focusing on the nature of the organization within the theory and practice of development, while on the other, there is an attempt to understand them by focusing on the nature of their response to that environment. This seemingly post-modernist approach is centered on the retreat from global concern for justice and international well-being, to more localized rapid response to local concerns. This is an issue to which I now turn in the next section.

NGDOs as organizations in the development context

As discussed in the previous sections, NGDOs evolve in historical contexts and to date, one cannot attempt the study of NGDOs without analyzing them as organizations operating in the context of development. Korten's[14] framework for analyzing NGDOs as organizations of change and adaptation adds a new dimension to our understanding of NGDOs. Over the past half a century, his analysis of the nature of NGDOs has resulted in a framework that locates these actors as evolving in phases or generations. Table 1.1 summarizes them.

In trying to further provide clarity to our understanding of NGDOs, Korten also talks about four classifications of NGDOs. These, according to his analysis, are: voluntary organizations; public service contractors; people's organizations; and governmental organizations (GONGOs). This classification is not only important in underscoring his notion of generations of "NGO development" but it is also essential as a starting point in understanding the diversity of these actors whose roles mutate with the changing external as well as internal environments. Some of them play an intermediary role while others are indigenous. Some are intermediary but at the same time bearing an international identity.

Korten's classification has paved the way to a more critical reflection of some of the stages theorized by others. For example, Ian Smillie[15] makes reference to a Johns Hopkins University study conducted by Salamon and Anheier which concluded that the most rational way of defining an organization is by using its structure and operations.[16] This

Table 1.1 NGO classification of phases

Phase	Role
Phase 1	Relief and welfare: in which NGOs delivered social services during the period of centre shortages
Phase 2	Community development: in which NGOs functioned as mobilizers of popular and governmental support in responding to locally based community projects
Phase 3	Sustainable systems development: in which the focus of NGOs shifted to subregional and national concerns (especially in the environmental areas)
Phase 4	People's movements: in which NGOs functioning as activists and educators seek to coalesce and energize self-management networks towards both national and global social development goals

Source: (David Korten, *Getting to the 21st Century: Voluntary Action and the Global Agenda* (West Hartford, Conn.: Kumarian Press, 1990, 117))

kind of suggestion has further resulted in another set of NGO evolutionary stages:

- *Community-based volunteerism*: requiring a high degree of personal involvement and responsibility for the delivery of social services;
- *Institutionalization*: where the responsibility remains with people but is expressed through the formation of associations that may complement services provided by government;
- *Professionalization*: where demands for services and other issues lead to federation and professionalization of associations and, often, to government funding or even to a replacement by government service; and
- *Welfare*: one in which society provides for all people's needs and charities then become redundant.[17]

While these stages are not necessarily discrete, Smillie acknowledges that NGOs' dependence on donor funding tends to reflect stage two (institutionalization) than stage three (professionalization). Nonetheless, it is rather hard to draw a clear line as their (NGDO) activities may also be characterized by features of stage one.

Further analysis of NGO generational stages has also been suggested by de Senillosa[18] who, reflecting on Korten's frameworks, suggests a re-description of the stages. De Senillosa's view is that NGO historical metamorphosis passes through such stages as welfare, development, partnership, and empowerment.

In summary these authors and others with interest in the role of the NGDO sector share a common view that underscores the fact that NGDOs, as organizations, have adaptive capacity to the changing nature of the development industry. Being closer to the reality of life gives them a comparative advantage (an issue we shall examine in more detail later in the book) over other stakeholders in the aid industry. As we have seen, the stages which NGDOs go through only give us an indication of a moment in time but the truth is that, in practice, NGDOs may operate or are likely to operate at two or more of these stages simultaneously. It is fair to acknowledge, therefore, that these frameworks work well when looked at as typologies of NGO activities rather than typologies of NGOs.

NGDOs in the development environment

The changing development and foreign aid landscape over the past two decades has reconfigured the way NGDOs operate. The global political landscape, reconceptualized by the ripple effects of globalization, has contributed to the reshaping of the way NGDOs operate.[19] International NGDOs in particular have been made to react to the expanding scale, growing magnitude, speeding up, and deepening impact of transcontinental flows and patterns of social interaction which, in essence, is globalization.[20]

From this perspective, NGDOs are understood more as responding to these challenges rather than being mere active players in shaping the ramifications of global forces. In this framework, the collapse of communism in Eastern Europe in the early 1980s and the rise of neoliberalism undergirded by a free market economy, have combined to shape today's NGDO sector. For international NGDOs, this global dynamism means they play a dual role—that of an intermediary between donors and recipients, and one in which international NGDOs have to provide aid as a panacea to global inequality or, put differently, that of representing an alternative to more human-centered development which the current civil society organizations highly espouse.[21]

Pearce specifically observes that while the advent of globalization has made the role of NGDOs and government more diffuse, "politically, there is the collapse of the reforming and revolutionary-left project, with its emphasis on state power. Economically, there is the rise of the neoliberal economics and its emphasis upon the retreat of the state and development led by the private sector."[22] While this is the case, NGDOs still have to negotiate their path through the political machinery of states as an institution mandated by its citizens. Viewed from this comparative advantage lens, it would appear that NGDOs are actors that are automatically accepted yet, by their definition, still remain awkwardly placed to claim the ascendancy beyond the state apparatus. This has created a situation where their place within the development industry remains uncertain.

Pearce further warns that NGDOs, while viewed as a solution to the future of the state apparatus, should not be analyzed as a singular entity with a common goal and characteristics because this is likely to conceal their strengths and more especially their weaknesses. As they scale-up their activities, the measure of their success may be compromised in the process. This analytical framework is useful in critically analyzing what NGDOs claim to do and what they actually do.

There is, however, a growing temptation in the analysis of NGDOs in the development context. As alluded to earlier, there is a growing demand for service in the Third World, but much of this need arises, at least in part, from the ripple effects of global politics. The question that arises is: can NGDOs deal with both or should they focus on one aspect? Bebbington, one of the development commentators, puts this into perspective when he argues that:

> NGOs have always been in part a response to state failure, in part a response to market failure, and in part a response to weaknesses in popular organizations. On some occasions, they have acted more like a state, other times more like an ally of the popular organization, and on other, though fewer occasions, more like a (socially orientated) market activator. This mixing of roles has never been easy, and has contributed to the crises that NGOs now face. In the future, one senses that NGOs will have increasingly to focus on one or other of these primary roles—and will in this way clarify the basis of their identity, legitimacy and financial security. As they do this, many following the first or second pathways will cease to be NGOs in the historical sense and should cease to be called such. This should not necessarily be seen as a problem. Indeed, it will probably be the way in which the validity and legitimacy of the denomination "NGO" will be sustained.[23]

Bebbington brings forth one major issue which the next section aims to articulate in more depth: the issue of financial security. Because of the fact that the tasks NGDOs set themselves to do are financially resource-demanding, they cannot do without aid, but how does that happen?

NGDOs and aid modalities

The philanthropic culture that existed in the early days of the non-profit sector, as discussed in the previous sections, is no longer the same. Most NGDOs today cannot survive without aid. However, the reality is that the transfer of resources from one point to another is a highly political process. John Davidson once said, "Aid is an intensely political act ... Aid is 10 percent technical and 90 percent political. This is why better leadership in local management is crucial to success, because it's about how politics works on the ground."[24] Similarly, the chairperson of the Institute for State Effectiveness, who is also a former minister of finance of Afghanistan, once said: "The design of aid is crucial for making it useful. The current system of aid is incapable of coordinating itself because of the 'NGO-Contractor-Security' model. Unless that model is tackled and host country budgets are the central mechanism for funds and policy making, aid will be constrained."[25] The sentiments of Ashraf Ghani and those of John Davidson above, underscore the politics behind foreign development assistance. As explored earlier, the changing social, economic and political contexts of both the developed and developing countries have given NGDOs an impetus to rise above the challenge of those in need. Undoubtedly, there seems to be a need for a moral crusade to do good. Today, NGDOs are highly dependent on funding from multilateral institutions such as the World Bank, European Union, UN, or bilateral donors such as the Australian Agency for International Development (AusAID), the UK Department for International Development (DfID), United States Agency for International Development (USAID), or Japan International Cooperation Agency (JICA), just to mention a few. It is becoming increasingly common for many local NGDOs also to be recipients of government funding, where their role becomes that of a government contractor. Their dependency on (foreign) donors has a direct influence on their moral crusade. Perhaps what has become a worrisome issue in this process is what seems to be a rigid institutionalized funding mechanism. The competition for funding, as a result of an ever-increasing number of NGDOs, reflects the number of funding bodies that currently exist. According to Lewis and Kanji, "There are currently more than 40 bilateral donor agencies, 26 UN agencies and a further 20 global and regional financial institutions involved in the system."[26]

How much money do NGDOs receive?

The amount of money the NGDO sector receives has been an issue of intense debate over the past decade and half, and continues to be so.[27] While there is a significant effort to assess how much aid is channeled through INGOs, data on how much aid is channeled through local NGOs is scarce, let alone published locally. Where it exists, the documents are sacred as secrets themselves. Nevertheless, indications are that in the early to mid-1990s, 12 percent of foreign aid to developing countries was channeled through NGOs.[28] Chege,[29] for example, estimates that as of 1996, NGOs managed over US$7 billion worldwide. Draher, Mölders and Nunnenkamp[30] also note that between 2005 and 2006, the share of bilateral overseas development assistance (ODA) managed by NGOs was in excess of 15 percent from various Organisation for Economic Co-operation and Development (OECD) countries. The share of total ODA by the Development Assistance Committee (DAC) countries channeled through NGOs has varied over the years, as indicated in Table 1.2.

In some countries like Australia, initiatives of enhancing aid effectiveness have been very positive. For example, on 20 June 2012, the

Table 1.2 Share of total ODA channeled through NGOs by DAC
countries 2008–09

Country	Percentage GNI
Australia	7.6
Austria	5.3
Belgium	11.5
Canada	10.8
Denmark	13.8
Finland	1.4
France	6.3
Germany	6.2
Greece	0.9
Ireland	38.5
Italy	2.5
Japan	1.7
South Korea	1.0
Luxembourg	16.9
Netherlands	20.2
New Zealand	11.2
Norway	–
Portugal	1.7
Spain	17.0
Sweden	12.6
Switzerland	11.7
United Kingdom	5.5
United States	–

Source: (OECD, Development Cooperation Directorate (November 2010),
www.oecd.org/dac/stats/38429349.pdf)

Australian government development branch, AusAID, launched the
"Civil Society Engagement Framework," which sets out how AusAID
will work with civil society, of which NGOs are a part. The main
objectives of this initiative are to:

• improve aid effectiveness and impact;
• enhance sustainability;
• reduce risk and share accountability;
• improve efficiency and value for money; and
• enhance diversity and encourage innovation.[31]

Over the years the rise in the number of INGOs has given a new
dimension to the aid architecture, with many of these INGOs playing
intermediary roles which fall in the category of a development provider
and/or a donor agency.[32] This dual role is not only problematic but

affirms the changing nature of the development industry. The multi-dimensionality of NGDOs is the subject of constant scrutiny. Within the past 10 years, books such as *The Change Imperative,*[33] *Snakes in Paradise: NGOs and the Aid Industry in Africa,*[34] *Non-Governmental Organizations and Development,*[35] *Can NGOs Make a Difference?*[36] *Between a Rock and a Hard Place: African NGOs, Donors and the State*[37] and many more, have been published to offer a critical reflection of the role of the development NGOs within the aid architecture. Considering their comparative advantages, state legitimacy and the political economy of aid itself, NGDOs' position in the broader aid industry can be described as complex and highly contestable.

What is even more pressing is that NGDOs rarely articulate their exit strategies.[38] The competing views of the recipients and the conditionalities imposed by the donor agencies are the two major issues that have caught the attention of commentators to study these actors more thoroughly. Besides, there is one fundamental question that continues to trouble commentators in the field of international development. Are NGDOs effective within the current aid architecture or, as Gilles Nancy and Boriana Yontcheva[39] ask, "does NGO aid go to the poor?" In order to respond to this question, the sections that follow examine the aid architecture and how, over the years, the debate has polarized commentators who study the political economy of foreign development assistance.

A brief history of aid

That aid is a divisive issue, has a long history.[40] It has often been said that aid creates dependency.[41] From colonization to the present era of Millennium Development Goals (MDGs), aid has been useful and harmful in many ways. On the one hand aid has surely been very useful in emergencies. However, on the other, it has created malaise among nations that have the potential to stand on their own. The intensity of the debate has, indeed, been polarizing. For example, the two camps of Peter Singer and Jeffrey Sachs (who are pro-aid) and that of Dambisa Moyo and William Easterly (who are skeptics) attest to the controversy surrounding the industry.[42] Despite this, though, the history of aid can be explained in eight phases, colonial era, post-war era, modernization and industrialization, decolonization, human approach, the Lost Decade of development, MDGs, and the Paris Declaration.[43]

Moyo[44] breaks the history of foreign aid into seven chronological sections: the Bretton Woods establishment in the 1940s; the era of the Marshall

Table 1.3 The history of aid

Era	Reason for aid
Colonization	Export of capital and manufactured goods in exchange for import, especially raw materials
	Loans from colonizers to the colonized not for ordinary citizens but for the urban elite
Post-war development, 1944–46	World Bank and other international financial institutions (IFIs) used as fundraiser for the reconstruction of Europe but later spilled over to developing countries
Modernization and industrialization era, 1949	Advancement of Truman doctrine: modernization of underdeveloped countries of the Third World
	Modernization and industrialization viewed as panacea for poverty reduction
Decolonization, 1959–1960s	Emergence of nations of developed vs. developing: the binaries that fortified the need for aid giving to enhance industrialization
Human needs approach, 1970s	Aid targeting social issues and services such as health, education, etc., rather than macro-economic growth
	Change from trickle-down philosophy to direct social service support
The Lost Decade of development, 1980s	Recession and debt crisis cause havoc in both developed and developing countries
	Aid targets structural reform through privatization and deregulation
Millennium Development Goals, 2000	Aid given in response to failures of growth-focused development approach
	Aid given to reduce poverty in targeted areas (see MDGs)
The Paris Declaration, 2005	Aid shifts from growth to effectiveness through ownership, alignment, harmonization, managing for results and mutual accountability

Source: (AIDWATCH, *Where is your Money Going?* aidwatch.org.au/where-is-your-aid-money-going)

Plan in the 1950s; the industrialization era of the 1960s; the shift in aid as an answer to poverty reduction in the 1970s; aid as a tool for structural adjustment and macro-economic stabilization in 1980; aid as a support mechanism for democracy and good governance in the 1990s; and aid as a panacea for the ills of the African continent in the millennium. A critical reflection on both AIDWATCH and Moyo brings to the fore John Davidson's sentiments—aid is highly political. The changing social, political, and economic environments dictate how aid can and should be used.

The aid debate outside NGDOs

While NGDOs are in the thick of foreign development assistance, we need to take a closer look at the aid debate in its entirety. As Arjan de Haan puts it, there is "The drama, the fiction" and the grand question: "Does it work?"[45] There is no question that aid is given with good intentions. It depends on who gives it, for what reason, and with or under what conditions. Ultimately, its well-intentioned outcome is to contribute to human well-being. At the center of all this, the final questions are: Has aid helped to improve the condition of the recipient target? Has it made any impact? How is this impact measured? In the absence of answers to some, if not all of these questions, what have become common are claims and counter-claims of whether aid works or not. At the end of the day, perhaps, we need to ask: Is it worth the crusade?

Since the implementation of one of the best known and probably the most successful aid program in the world—The Marshall Plan— development aid debate has received a lot of attention and scrutiny, often ending up with inconclusive answers. George Mavrotas[46] acknowledges the changes that have ensued since then and comments on some of the critical questions that have been raised over the past half a century, the answers to which remain elusive. On the one hand there are analysts who are from an economics side of the debate whose passion for quantitative analyses cannot be halted. On the other is a camp whose view of success is very much qualitative and much closer to the reality of life on the ground. Merging the two camps is an issue of Mavrotas's edited volume *Foreign Aid for Development*, which has polarized the aid effectiveness debate. While attempts have been made to provide concrete answers on aid effectiveness, the evidence on the ground has had a varied impact, as even the lauded MDG targets are far from being met by 2015.[47] For example, Oxfam records that in 2007, 9 million children under the age of five died from preventable diseases.[48] Furthermore, every year 350,000 women and girls die of complications emerging from childbearing. The majority are from the developing world.

The intensity of the current debate is an indication of the complexity of the development field, especially with reference to aid modalities. For those who argue against aid ineffectiveness, the arguments have been that aid encourages economic dependency, stunts economic growth, encourages corruption and laziness.[49] However, while these reasons are valid, the optimists point out that without aid, 4 million people who depend on aid for HIV/AIDS treatment would be dead. In addition, there are now 33 million more children whose access to schooling has been enhanced. This comes against the backdrop of missed MDG targets in many of the developing countries. While in recent years the international donor community has taken a step in the right direction by drawing lessons from around the world—by linking aid to results, opening channels of accountability and transparency, instilling fiscal discipline through governance structures—the $200 billion industry still reels with myriad challenges. Where are we getting it wrong? The next section takes the issue further by examining some of the issues on aid conditionality, the Paris Declaration and how the NGDO sector operationalizes them.

NGDOs and aid conditionality

> As you know, civil society groups have often expressed concerns about the IMF's [International Monetary Fund] conditionality policy. We have, in the past, worked tirelessly to address the poverty and social impacts that can be the result of IMF programs in borrowing countries. As you may know some civil society groups disagreed with the IMF methodology and classification, as spelled out in the 2008 Eurodad Report "*Critical conditions.*" It found out that since the conditionality guidelines were approved, the IMF had not managed to decrease the number of structural conditions and continued to make heavy use of highly sensitive conditions, such as privatization and liberalization.[50]

The concerns raised in the extract of a letter addressed to the IMF signed by Peter Chowla (program manager of the Bretton Woods Project), Nuria Molina (director of Eurodad) and Bhumika Muchhala (of the Third World Network), in 2010, on impending IMF conditionality review, underscore one of the most contentious issues in the development debate. NGDOs and borrowing governments often have to adhere to policy prescriptions that come as a package with aid. While indeed some measures are necessary to ensure that there is no wastage of resources by recipient governments or NGDOs, the majority of donors impose specific conditions that counter the key purpose for which aid is intended. For example, aid has always been tagged against fiscal and monetary choices. Other conditionalities have pushed governments to privatize public institutions and liberalize trade. It is the impact of these conditionalities that are a bone of contention and with which the NGDOs find themselves grappling, either as direct beneficiaries themselves or as they play intermediary roles between donors and their constituencies.

One of the popular debates in the current aid conditionality debate is "tying of aid" to, say, procurement.[51] Data on how much aid is tied to NGO work remain difficult to gather but a glimpse of this in Table 1.4, based on country data, provides some idea of how pervasive the issue is in international development.

The data presented here are predominantly based on bilateral aid—government to government. There is limited empirical evidence on the impact of donor conditionalities on NGDO work. However, Tina Wallace and Jenny Chapman[52] recount the experience of British NGOs, citing that part of the conditionalities imposed on them were tied to contracts for which NGOs bid. These contracts were based on donor strategic priorities, criteria and guidelines. In some cases the conditionalities directly affected NGO operations. Some of these operations were, for example, completing projects in a specified period of

Table 1.4 Tied aid by donors, 2008 (%)

Number	Donor	Tied share (%)
1	Greece	62
2	South Korea	57
3	Spain	30
4	United States	25
5	Italy	20
6	France	18
7	Austria	18
8	Portugal	11
9	Belgium	8
10	Canada	8
11	Finland	8
12	New Zealand	7
13	Netherlands	7
14	Japan	4
15	Australia	3
16	Switzerland	3
17	Germany	2
18	Denmark	1
19	Sweden	0
20	Norway	0
21	Ireland	0
22	Luxembourg	0
23	United Kingdom	0

Source: (OECD, in Todd J. Moss, *African Development: Making Sense of the Issues and Actors*, 2nd edn (Boulder, Col.: Lynne Rienner Publishing, 2011), 151)

Note: Some of the statistics may have changed over time as some of the countries like Australia are claiming to have completely "untied" their aid.

time and streamlining NGO proposals at the decision-making stages. For NGOs that acted as intermediaries between donors and beneficiaries, the same conditions were passed on to them.

It has to be noted that while the debate on conditionalities has been divisive, conditionalities have to be looked at from a broader context of who benefits from them. On the one hand, the debate on making poverty history is about enhancing development effectiveness—that is, how to ensure that development is sustainable. On the other, the aid effectiveness debate is about producing results, essentially based on stand-alone development projects. It is the latter category in which NGDOs find themselves. Because many development NGOs are donor dependent for their operations, by inference they are largely influenced by these conditionalities to the extent that very often their original plans get shifted as they continue to negotiate approval for and how to put the projects into effect.

Tying aid to national interests is very common in food aid. For example, US Public Law 480, also known as "Food For Peace" (FFP), is the funding mechanism through which US food can be incorporated into overseas aid packages. Cunningham notes that food aid is part of a larger phenomenon called "tied aid," which must be spent within the donor country.[53] For example, 93 percent of USAID funding is tied and in 2012 USAID awarded 59 percent of its $14.5 billion in foreign assistance spending to US contractors. The sentiments by Mark Ward, the director of the Office of Foreign Disaster Assistance, provide a nuanced view of the debate:

> The United States Government, through USAID, requires the NGOs we fund to "brand" the assistance they provide to people in need with the Agency's handshake, logo and the words "From the American people" in local languages. Branding is not just required by law; it ensures transparency when America provides aid. We believe that the people we help have a right to know where their assistance is coming from.[54]

A study by Busiinge[55] provides some insight into how donor conditionalities can adversely impact on NGO work. The Kabarole Research and Resource Centre (KRRC) in Rwenzori subregion in Uganda has a long history of working with donors. For a long time KRRC has been implementing a variety of development projects. Busiinge's project was set to understand the nature and origin of projects, the impact of donor-aided projects through KRRC on the social and economic well-being of grassroots communities, sustainability of donor-aided projects, and the kind of challenges and opportunities of such projects. The findings are consistent with broader development literature. For example, the study revealed that donors find it hard to operate outside the box. A good example cited is the use of logframes. While, for example, one would expect some flexibility in the implementation of projects based on monitoring data, donors are reported to have been very rigid in adjusting and accommodating new views and innovation. Ironically, the NGOs involved in implementing such projects could not do anything for fear of losing funding.

The food aid and the KRRC case study are vital in understanding the complexity of the politics of aid. Branding or no branding, flexibility of not, at the heart of the matter lie issues of power. Even when one locates the debate within the context where the flow of resources is from donors to recipients (NGDOs), the major issue is "control."

Conclusion

The purpose of this chapter was to examine the evolution of the NGO sector and how this evolution has resulted in the kind of NGO that is actively involved in development today. The growth of the NGDO sector has undergone a period of progressive change. In the early days, these organizations were formed to respond not only to humanitarian issues but also socio-political issues in the form of religious orders, societies, confederations, alliances and movements. The coalescing between the secular and religious institutions highlighted the importance and criticality of the issues the organizations addressed, but over time, some of the global dynamics have forced this early generation of NGDOs to reconfigure their focus. It is critically important that while it is vital that we understand the historical context in which they have evolved, we should also pay attention to the fact that the analytical frameworks that have been used to analyze the evolution of these organizations have their own limitations. It could be argued, therefore, that NGDOs are acting in, and are also acted upon by, their contexts.

The chapter has further highlighted that the changes that have been taking place since the end of the world wars have necessitated the reconfiguration of how NGDOs deal with some of the emerging issues. This change has meant that many NGDOs have moved into more service provision with increased dependency on funding from external donors. This means entering into relationships with competing interests, motives and accountabilities. The requirement to meet certain conditions before funding is approved has been the hallmark of the new aid modalities. The call for most aid policies to align with other stakeholders in order to enhance aid effectiveness is not a simple issue. In Chapter 2, I delve deep into the issues of partnerships in order to tease out how NGDOs work with other stakeholders when they are largely dependent on external funding.

Notes

1 Kevin C. Robbins, "The Nonprofit Sector in Historical Perspective: Tradition of Philanthropy in the West," in *The Non-Profit Sector: A Research Handbook*, 2nd edn, ed. Walter W. Powell and Richard Steinberg (New Haven, Conn. and London: Yale University Press, 2003), 13–31.
2 J. Lane, S. Saxon-Harold and N. Weber, *International Giving and Volunteering* (London: Charities Aid Foundation, 1994).
3 David Lewis and Nankeen Kanji, *Non-Governmental Organizations and Development* (London: Routledge, 2009), 30.
4 theglobaljournal.net/article/view/981/.
5 theglobaljournal.net/article/view/981/.
6 Thomas R. Davies, *The Rise and Fall of Transnational Civil Society: The Evolution of International Non-Governmental Organizations since 1839* (April 2008), www.staff.city.ac.uk/tom.davies/CUWPTP003.pdf.
7 Davies, *The Rise and Fall of Transnational Civil Society*; for more on this, see Bob Reinalda, *Routledge History of International Organizations: From 1815 to the Present Day* (London: Routledge, 2009).
8 Davies, *The Rise and Fall of Transnational Civil Society*.
9 Davies, *The Rise and Fall of Transnational Civil Society*, 4.
10 R.A. Couto, "Community Coalitions and Grassroots Policies of Empowerment," *Administration and Society* 30, no. 5 (1998): 569–94; Lester M. Salamon and Helmut K. Anheier, "The Third World's Third Sector Comparative Advantage," in *International Perspectives on Voluntary Action: Reshaping the Third Sector*, ed. David Lewis (London: Earthscan, 1999): 60–93; Dorothea Hilhorst, *The Real World of NGOs: Discourse, Diversity and Development* (London: Zed Books, 2003); Steven J. Klees, "NGOs, Civil Society, and Development: Is there a Third Way?" *Current Issues in Comparative Education* 10, nos. 1 & 2 (2008): 22–25.
11 Salamon and Anheier, "The Third World's Third Sector Comparative Advantage."
12 Hilhorst, *The Real World of NGOs*.
13 Salamon and Anheier, "The Third World's Third Sector Comparative Advantage."
14 David Korten, *Getting to the 21st Century: Voluntary Action and the Global Agenda* (West Hartford, Conn.: Kumarian Press, 1990).
15 Ian Smillie, *The Arms Bazaar* (London: Intermediate Technology Publications, 1995).
16 Salamon and Anheier, "The Third World's Third Sector Comparative Advantage."
17 Smillie, *The Arms Bazaar*.
18 Ignacio de Senillosa, "A New Age of Social Movements: A Fifth Generation of Non-Governmental Organizations in the Making," *Development in Practice* 8, no. 1 (February 1998): 40–52.

19 Susan M. Roberts, John P. Jones III and Oliver Fröhling, "NGOs and the Globalization of Managerialism: A Research Framework," *World Development* 33, no. 11 (2005): 1845–64; Barbara Rugendyke, ed., *NGOs as Advocates for Development in Globalized World* (London and New York: Routledge, 2007).

20 Paul Ronalds, *The Change Imperative: Creating the Next Generation NGO* (Sterling, Va.: Kumarian Press, 2010).

21 Alan Fowler, *Partnerships: Negotiating Relationships: A Resource for Non-Governmental Development Organizations*, INTRAC Occasional Papers No. 32 (Oxford: INTRAC, 2000); Michael Edwards and David Hulme, "NGOs and Development: Performance and Accountability in the New World Order," background paper for the international workshop on "NGOs and Development: Performance and Accountability in the New World Order," University of Manchester, 27–29 June 1994.

22 Jenny Pearce, "NGOs and Social Change: Agents or Facilitators?" *Development in Practice* 3, no. 3 (1993): 223.

23 Anthony Bebbington, "New States, New NGOs? Crises and Transitions among Rural Development NGOs in the Andean Region," *World Development* 25, no. 11 (1997): 1764.

24 Kemal Dervis, Homi Kharas and Nnoam Unger, *Aiding Development: Assistance Reform for 21st Century* (Brookings Plum Roundtable, 2010), 8, www.brookings.edu/~/media/research/files/reports/2011/2/02%20aiding%20d evelopment/02_aiding_development.pdf.

25 Dervis, Kharas and Unger, *Aiding Development*, 13.

26 Lewis and Kanji, *Non-Governmental Organizations and Development*, 30.

27 Sam Chege, "Donors Shift More Aid to NGOs," *Africa Recovery* 13, no. 1 (1999):6; Dirk-Jan Koch, Axel Dreher, Peter Nunnenkamp and Rainer Thiele, *Keeping a Low Profile: What Determines the Allocation of Aid by Non-Governmental Organizations?* KOF Working Papers (March 2008), www.econstor.eu/dspace/bitstream/10419/28935/1/584001886.pdf; Karen Rauh, "NGOs, Foreign Donors, and Organizational Processes: Passive NGO Recipients or Strategic Actors?" *McGill Sociological Review* 1, no. 1 (2010): 29–45; Nicole Banks and David Hulme, *The Role of NGOs and Civil Society in Development and Poverty Alleviation*, Brooks World Poverty Institute, Working Paper 171 (Manchester: Brooks World Poverty Institute, 2012).

28 World Bank, *Assessing Aid: What Works, What Doesn't, and Why* (Oxford: Oxford University Press, 1998).

29 Chege, "Donors Shift More Aid to NGOs."

30 Alex Draher, Florian Mölders and Peter Nunnenkamp, *Are NGOs the Better Donors? A Case Study of Aid Allocation for Sweden*, Kiel Working Paper No. 1383 (October 2007), www.ifw-members.ifw-kiel.de/publications/are-ngos-the-better-donors-a-case-study-of-aid-allocation-for-sweden/kap13 83.pdf.

31 AusAID, *AusAID NGO Cooperation Program: Monitoring, Evaluation and Learning Framework* (June 2012), p. iv, www.ausaid.gov.au/ngos/Document s/ancp-program.pdf.

32 Jonathan J. Makuwira, "Development? Freedom? Whose Development and Freedom?" *Development in Practice* 16, no. 2 (2006): 193–200; Terje Tvedt, "The International Aid System and the Non-Governmental Organizations: A New Research Agenda," *Journal of International Development* 18, no. 5

(2006): 677–90; Hans Holmén, *Snakes in Paradise: NGOs and the Aid Industry in Africa* (Sterling, Va.: Kumarian Press, 2010); Paul Ronalds, *The Change Imperative: Creating the Next Generation NGO* (Sterling, Va.: Kumarian Press, 2010).

33 Ronalds, *The Change Imperative*.
34 Holmén, *Snakes in Paradise*.
35 Lewis and Kanji, *Non-Governmental Organizations and Development*.
36 Anthony J. Bebbington, Sam Hickey and Diana Mitlin, eds, *Can NGOs Make a Difference? The Challenge of Development Alternatives* (London: Zed Books, 2008).
37 Jim Igoe and Tim Kelsall, *Between a Hard Rock and a Hard Place: African NGOs, Donors, and the State* (Durham, N.C.: Carolina Academic Press, 2005).
38 Derek Fee, *How to Manage an Aid Exit Strategy: The Future of Development Aid* (London: Zed Books, 2012).
39 Gilles Nancy and Boriana Yontcheva, "Does NGO Aid Go to the Poor? Empirical Evidence from Europe," *IMF Working Paper* WP/06/39 (February 2006), www.hapinternational.org/pool/files/wp0639.pdf.
40 Dambisa Moyo, *Dead Aid: Why Aid is Not Working and How there is a Better Way for Africa* (New York: Farrar, Straus and Giroux, 2009).
41 Jonathan Glennie, *The Trouble with Aid: Why Less Could Mean More* (London: Zed Books, 2008); Moyo, *Dead Aid*; Todd J. Moss, *African Development: Making Sense of the Issues and Actors*, 2nd edn (Boulder, Co.: Lynne Rienner Publishing, 2011).
42 See, for example, issues raised by Wolfgang Fingler and Homi Kharas, "Delivering Aid Differently: Lessons from the Field," *World Economic Premise* 49 (February 2011), siteresources.worldbank.org/INTPREMNET/Resources/EP49.pdf.
43 AIDWATCH, *Where is your Money Going?* aidwatch.org.au/where-is-your-aid-money-going.
44 Moyo, *Dead Aid*.
45 Arjan de Haan, "Aid: The Drama, the Fiction, and Does it Work?" *ISS Working Paper No. 488* (December 2009), repub.eur.nl/res/pub/18705/wp488.pdf.
46 George Mavrotas, *Foreign Aid for Development: Issues, Challenges, and the New Agenda* (London: Oxford University Press, 2010).
47 Robert Cassen and Associates, *Does Aid Work?* 2nd edn, (Oxford: Oxford University Press, 1994); Roger Riddell, *Does Foreign Aid Really Work?* (Oxford: Oxford University Press, 2007); George Mavrotas and Mark McGillivray, eds., *Development Aid: A Fresh Look* (Basingstoke: Palgrave Macmillan, 2009); Moyo, *Dead Aid*; Oxfam, *21st Century Aid: Recognizing Success and Tackling Failure*, Oxfam Briefing Paper 137 (April 2010), www.oxfam.org/sites/www.oxfam.org/files/bp137–21st-century-aid-summary.pdf.
48 Oxfam, *21st Century Aid*, 5.
49 Oxfam, *21st Century Aid*, 5.
50 Peter Chowla, Nuria Molina, Bhumika Muchhala, Soren Ambrose, Bernice Romero, "2011 Conditionality Review," a letter submitted to Reza Moghadam, Director SPR Department, International Monetary Fund (IMF), 13 December 2010.
51 Oliver Cunningham, "The Humanitarian Aid Regime in the Republic of NGOs: The Fallacy of 'Building Back Better'," *The Josef Korbel Journal of Advanced International Studies* 4 (2012): 102–29.

52 Tina Wallace and Jenny Chapman, *Is the Way Aid is Disbursed through NGOs Promoting a Development Practice that Addresses Chronic Poverty Well? An Overview of an On-going Research Project* (2003), www.chronic poverty.org/uploads/publication_files/CP_2003_Wallace_Chapman.pdf.
53 Cunningham, "The Humanitarian Aid Regime in the Republic of NGOs."
54 Mark Ward, USAID Assistance to Pakistan (October 2010), blog.usaid.gov/ 2010/10/usaid-assistance-in-pakistan/, cited in Cunningham, "The Humanitarian Aid Regime in the Republic of NGOs," 105.
55 Christopher Busiinge, *The Impact of Donor Aided Projects through NGOs on the Social and Economic Welfare of the Rural Poor: What do the Donors Want? Case Study: Kabarole Research & Resource Centre* (June 2010), www.rgs.org/NR/rdonlyres/3200ECC1-391E-43F6-A89F-2212F856F449/0/ BUSIINGERESEARCHRGSCopy.pdf.

2 The moral case for partnerships

- Understanding the idea of "partnership"
- Partnerships between NGDOs and states
- Factors affecting NGDO-state partnerships
- Partnerships between and among NGOs
- NGOs and community partnerships
- Conclusion

The NGO moral crusade to reduce poverty is marred by the language of partnerships. As the context of development aid is constantly changing, the reality of "going it alone" is under constant review. Over the past two decades, numerous development discourses have entered center stage of the development lexicon. Among these discourses, the term "partnership" has been widely discussed without a conclusive end to the tensions and contradictions inherent in both its conceptual underpinnings and practical application.[1] Framed in the context of current aid architecture, the idea has become a bone of contention in highlighting the balance between rhetoric and reality. For NGDOs, the idea is an insidious bedfellow in their quest to garner support for their development endeavors. The NGDOs' active role as service providers has not only led to their encounter with multiple development actors but has also exerted a lot of pressure on how they manage these multiple realities.

The aim of this chapter is to analyze critically the discourse of "partnership" by unpacking competing theoretical underpinnings and relating them to how such theoretical principles are applied in practice. The chapter also provides a snapshot of various models of partnerships between NGDOs and states, NGDOs and other NGDOs both from the "north" and "south," and NGDOs and their intended beneficiaries.

Understanding the idea of "partnership"

The term "partnership" has different connotations. In some instances terms such as collaboration, cooperation, coordination or relationship have been used to denote a partnership of some kind. Various development theorists[2] have attempted to navigate through the various meanings of the concept. Fowler,[3] in particular, eloquently argues that the term "partnership" is aimed to mean strategic alliances or coalitions between two or more entities that are actively involved in a particular activity with a shared vision of achieving a common goal. Given the fluidity of the concept, Fowler[4] takes the definition further by pointing out that an "authentic partnership implies ... a joint commitment to a long-term intervention, shared responsibility for achievement, reciprocal obligation, equality, mutuality and balance of power."

In development circles, the idea that partnerships engender positive results can be far-fetched. Looking at the definitions above one easily notices the emphasis on power relationships. The fact that NGDOs heavily rely on external funding to carry out their development activities throws the whole notion of partnership into microscopic scrutiny. Reed and Reed[5] caution that the existence of unequal power relationships in a given structure entails that the elites in these structures amass and control resources which provide them with structural power. For organizations and institutions engaged in development, these observations highlight and underscore one of the challenges of development—the unequal power relations that are manifested in institutions and practices which often combine to constitute larger social, political and economic structures.[6]

Cautious as we may be in engaging in any form of partnerships, the literature on effective partnerships hinges, it seems, on the principles of:

- mutuality;
- respect;
- equality in decision-making processes;
- clearly defined goals;
- influences;
- expectations;
- maintenance of organizational identity;
- rights and responsibilities;
- equitable distribution of costs and benefits;
- accountability to the primary beneficiaries; and
- transparency.[7]

While these principles sound rosy and are widely acknowledged as guiding pillars to effective partnerships, there is limited evidence on how various models of partnerships work on the ground.[8] Where these partnerships are studied, there is weak application of methodological and theoretical rigor. McLoughlin[9] aptly argues that the complex nature of the state-NGO relationship, for example, is poorly understood, often simplified and lacks a firm theoretical basis. The literature is often described as prescriptive, incomplete, and even anecdotal or dominated by subjective accounts of selected use of case studies largely produced within the NGO community. The sections that follow explore various forms of partnerships and how they are operationalized in practice.

Partnerships between NGDOs and states

The debate on the relationship between NGDOs and states has always been a contentious one.[10] In part NGDOs' legitimacy and representivity is a good starting point. The NGDOs' behavior, as they operate within the confines of state, dictates the nature and quality of their relationships with states. Given that NGDOs operate in a world polity fundamentally ordered by states, it is vital that we gain a fair understanding of the basic principles that dictate NGDO-state relationships. For development-oriented NGOs, the "nongovernmental" phraseology is no excuse to undermine state legitimacy. Moreover, development is political, hence any attempt by NGDOs to legitimate their actions under the guise of their independence not only breeds antagonism but can also obscure their contribution to the government's development efforts. Let us take the case of Malawi, where over the past three decades there have been twists and turns in the relationship between government and civil society organizations (CSOs).

Box 2.1 Case study: government of Malawi-civil society partnerships

Since gaining independence in 1964 from the British government, Malawi's leadership has defined its relationships with CSOs in different ways. During Kamuzu Banda's era (1964–94), the existence of CSOs was limited to service provision. In particular, faith-based organizations dominated the practice with only a handful engaged in other sectors. Because of the fact that Banda's regime was dictatorial, dissent was suppressed. Only one political party existed, thus defining the boundaries between states and non-state actors and, crucially, civic engagement in political affairs of the country.

The second phase of Malawi's post-independence era (1994–2004), saw a regime that was different from that of Dr Banda. The Bakili Muluzi era witnessed a style of leadership that accommodated CSOs which, according to Rogge,[1] was "to build an open society governed by democratic rules and institutions which encourage(d) participation of individuals, groups and communities in the political, social, economic and human development of the country." Indeed the 10 years of his rule enabled the burgeoning of the CSO sector engaged in various development activities. However, the awareness of democratic principles raised during this period proved politically lethal when, towards the end of his second term in office, Muluzi decided to fiddle around with the Constitution in order to allow him to rule the country beyond the two five-year terms. The success of CSOs in curbing the would-be second wave of dictatorial regime was a perfect platform for the future role of CSOs in the third leadership regime.

The change in leadership from Bakili Muluzi to Bingu Wa Mutharika (2004–12) hardly disrupted the enabling environment within which CSOs were operating. The first term of Wa Mutharika's presidency was predicated on strengthening the role of CSOs in civic engagement. On numerous occasions CSOs have been engaged in government policy debates, although with some frustrations due to limitations imposed by government in some instances. However, since Mutharika won the presidential and parliamentary elections in 2009 in a landslide, the regime went on the rampage, passing some controversial legislation in parliament. One example of such legislation was Section 46 of the Penal Code of the Constitution of Malawi (CAP 7:01), which granted sweeping powers to the minister of information to ban any publications deemed not to be in the public interest. This anti-media freedom opened a wave of attacks and criticism from CSOs with some newspapers bearing titles such as:

- Civil society demand withdrawal of government threats on private media;
- Malawi CSOs rip Mutharika tirade;
- Mutharika refuses to step down, "DPP to rule Malawi beyond 2023"; and
- Mutharika's seven-point deadline extended.

The bone of contention between government and CSOs in Malawi gravitated around issues of governance, transparency, accountability and the rule of law. For example, the interview between CIVICUS and Billy Mayaya, program manager of "church and society" of the Church of Central African Presbyterians (CCAP), Nkhoma Synod, offers some insights.

CIVICUS: The environment for civil society in Malawi appears to be deteriorating for the past few months. Could you tell us a little bit about the current situation and your recent arrest with four other colleagues?

MAYAYA: There is an incremental movement towards shrinking civil society space in Malawi, the dynamics of which were prompted by the current ruling party's landslide victory in 2009. The Democratic Progressive Party viewed this as license to rule without the consensus of the people that voted them into power for a second term. Concerned with the increasing levels of impunity, civil society as a collective began to demand transparency, accountability and observance of the rule of law. In response, the position of government was to maintain a more hard-line approach. This was evidenced by the level of vitriol directed to civil society concerns. Civil society organisations and select individuals were publicly targeted at presidential functions as being agents of foreign governments bent on damaging Malawi's profile abroad. Civil society organisations were branded a security risk and threatened with deregistration. As a response, the Government has enacted legislation meant to further shrink the space for civil society. Chief among these is the NGO Act 2000 which cautions NGO not to engage in political activities a veiled reference to advocacy.

Currently, the political and economic situation is worsening by the day. Fuel and forex [foreign exchange] shortages are negatively affecting Malawi's already fragile socio-political status. Civil servants spend months on end without being paid. Local government elections have not been held since the year 2000 thus depriving ordinary citizens of their right to develop at the local level. Civil society drew a 20 point petition demanding among other things that the President explain his ill-gotten wealth and desalarise the First Lady's salary of US$10000 a month for charitable work. If these issues were not addressed, we warned that we would organize nationwide demonstrations to show our displeasure. In July, peaceful demonstrations were held. The

government responded by shooting 20 people dead. We condemned this act of wanton savagery in the strongest terms and
insisted that we would not be deterred to hold more demonstra-
tions until the demands in the petition were adequately addressed.

We saw an opportunity to demonstrate at the COMESA
[Common Market for Eastern and Southern Africa] Heads of
State meeting which was to be held in Lilongwe in mid October.
On the day of our arrest, we carried a banner that read NO TO
DICACTORSHIP [sic]! WE DEMAND GOOD POLITICAL
AND ECONOMIC GOVERNANCE! BINGU IS A DIC-
TATOR! We were also nauseated by the presence of President
Omar al Bashir of North Sudan, currently wanted by the
International Criminal Court for genocide in Darfur. After
demonstrating, we were promptly arrested by undercover
police and denied police bail, which is guaranteed by Malawi's
Republican Constitution after 48 hours. We were kept in cus-
tody for six days. After a court appearance, we were charged
with conducting an illegal demonstration as well as sedition.
We are currently out on bail and will appear in court on the 25
November 2011.

Note

1 Tony Rogge, *A Brief Overview of the NGO Sector in Malawi: Options for CIDA Programming* (Malawi: Blantyre, 1997), 3.

(Jonathan J. Makuwira, "Civil Society Organizations (CSOs) and the Changing Nature of African Politics: The Case of the CSO–Government Relationship in Malawi," *Journal of Asian and African Studies* 46, no. 6 (2011): 615–28; CIVICUS, 2011, www.civicus.org/news-and-resources-127/658-civicus-interview-with-billy-mayaya.

The case study of the Malawi-CSO relationship offers some insights
into the complex terrain that both NGDOs and states constantly have to
navigate and, at the same time, negotiate. Ahmed and Potter[11] remind
us that NGDOs cannot replace states. States exist because of their
contractual arrangement with the citizenry through the ballot box. As
such, any attempt by NGDOs to play a "watchdog" role is often met
with resistance. The general observation is that states easily accommodate NGDOs that are "working dogs." In this category, NGDOs

are often cooperative and exhibit a complementary role to state development endeavors.

Barber and Bowie[12] have argued that many NGOs have sold themselves to donors in the name of independence. The fundamental question that follows this observation is: Can all NGDOs be independent? Taking an example of an NGO working in humanitarian emergencies, we can discuss the motive—that of allowing them to operate freely in all areas of critical need. Likewise, "independence" of development NGDOs is based on the need to depoliticize development and, more crucially, distance themselves from the political manipulation of governments of the day.[13] That said, the rapid burgeoning of the NGDO sector, in some instances, poses a dilemma to the state as NGDOs diversify their scope of operations and encapsulate virtually every aspect of human need. This is a moral ground on which NGDOs operate. In such a case, the form of relationships between NGDOs and governments that best facilitates sustainable development becomes complex. Therefore, the nature and model of NGDO-government partnership adopted matters most and below I attempt to highlight them.

In their seminal work on the third sector and government relations, Gidron, Kramer and Salamon[14] identify four types of NGO-government relations. This typology demonstrates the complexity that exists when we broadly analyze NGDOs operating within the confines of states.

Other topologies are those that are purely dualistic in nature. For example, there are relationships that can be seen as "strong–weak,"[15] "formal–informal,"[16] and "active–dependent."[17]

The work of Coston[18] takes the work of Gidron and his colleagues a little further and offers a comprehensive model and typology that best encapsulates most of the current thinking. Over the years, her work has been adapted based on prevailing social, economic and political contexts. The thrust of the model and typology is based on eight relationship types, the dimensions of which are characterized by:

- government resistance or acceptance of institutional pluralism;
- the balance of power;
- degree of formality and/or informality in the relationship; and
- level of linkages (often an extension of the informality).

Coston, like other commentators,[19] focuses on a normative interpretation of these models, highlighting that oftentimes government-NGO models have to be understood not only from an organizational form and behavior but also from the influence of history, legal definitions, culture, state policies and functions, and origin and behavior of NGDOs themselves.

Table 2.1 Models of NGO partnerships with other stakeholders

Partnership model	Features
Government dominant model	Government plays a dominant role in financing and delivery of services Government uses taxpayer's money to find various services delivered by government employees
Third sector dominant model	NGDOs play a dominant role in financing and delivery of services NGDOs sector plays a "watchdog" role over governments
Dual model (parallel track model)	NGDOs play a supplementary role by providing services to marginalized sections of communities not reached by governments. NGDOs are gap fillers
Collaborative model	NGDOs and governments work together on an intervention common to their strategic direction NGDOs act as agents of government programming (collaborative-Vendor-Model) or NGDOs engage in a contractual arrangement while maintaining some degree of autonomy

Source: (Adapted from Benjamin Gidron, Ralph Kramer and Lester Salamon, "Government and the Third Sector in Comparative Perspective: Allies or Adversaries?" in *Government and the Third Sector: Emerging Relationships in Welfare States*, ed. Benjamin Godron, Ralph Kramer and Lester Salamon (San Francisco, Calif.: Jossey-Bass Publishers, 1992); Terje Tvedt, *Angels of Mercy or Development Diplomats? NGOs and Foreign Aid* (Trenton: African World Press, 1998))

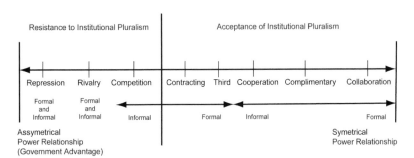

Figure 2.1 Typology of partnerships: the government-NGO relationship (Jennifer M. Coston, "A Model and Typology of Government-NGO Relationships", *Nonprofit and Voluntary Sector Quarterly* 27, no. 3 (1998): 363)

While it is highly unlikely that NGDO-government relationships will mirror purely one of these models, governments are at liberty to engage or disengage from any form of relationship. This was typified by the state of affairs in Malawi where, while there were efforts by both parties to come to agreement, the government decided to walk away because of what it considered unreasonable demands. As Jones[20] posits, states remain principal actors in development. Although NGDOs are accommodated by state apparatus in the negotiation, identification, implementation, monitoring and evaluation of development programs, their inclusion in these critical decision-making processes does not come at the expense of state authority. Rather, clever governments use their legitimacy to engage NGDOs as a utility to social service provision endeavors. It is clear that in this scenario NGDOs have to acknowledge the fact that governments/ states control the rules of the game based on international instruments. In the words of Raustiala,[21] "NGO access to international organizations is not an inalienable right, and thus NGOs['] participation remains a privilege granted and mediated by states."

Lately, there is an acknowledgement of the dynamism that exists when analyzing NGDO-state relationships. Indeed, while the state may exhibit a custodial stance against NGDO operation, on the other hand NGDOs do also exercise agency in shaping their agenda as they continually interact with states. Adil Najam,[22] for example, offers a word of caution, that our attempts to understand NGDO-state relationships should be situated within the "push"–"pull" factor. In this context, Najam argues that both parties may exercise institutional choices as each one of them pursues their own goals and strategies. For example, organizations may decide to cooperate because they share similar ends and means. In other instances, they complement each other purely because they share similar ends but not necessarily similar means. In other cases, co-optation may occur because they have similar means but differ in their goals. In an extreme case organizations may be in confrontation because they share neither ends nor means. It is from these analytical frameworks that our analysis of NGDO-state partnerships should be premised on the belief that neither NGDOs nor states are monolithic; hence, their relationships are constantly dynamic.

Box 2.2 Case study: Homa Hills Community Development Organization and the Government of Kenya Partnership on Early Childhood Education and Development

Homa Hills Community Development Organization (HHCDO), a child-centered NGO, was initially established in 1980 as an agricultural center by the Norwegian Save the Children. Its transition from the original mission to one focusing on low school enrollment in schools gave the organization a platform on which to collaborate with the government of Kenya on Early Childhood Education and Development (ECED). The partnership was one based on common concern, trust and mutuality. The common concern between the two entities was human resources: teachers. The HHCDO offered to support the identification of community members to be trained as teachers in order to support their mission. The organization targeted women whom they believed would stay in the area after receiving training, unlike men who have to leave the area for marriage elsewhere. On its part, the government offered space at its training center for HHCDO for community-based teachers to be trained. Furthermore, the government of Kenya mounted a campaign to raise awareness on the importance of ECED. While the program experienced isolation by the formal primary schools, due to lack of knowledge of the importance of ECED, it later turned out to be a success as HHCDO continued to provide support in primary schools as an agenda to promulgate messages of the importance of ECED.

Achievements

The project manager is proud of what HHCDO has been able to achieve over the years. Enrollment in the ECD centers is at an all-time high and community members are now sold on the need to provide ECED for their children. He points to the fact that community members currently come to the schools on a voluntary basis to prepare porridge for the children as a major plus for the program.

Every year, HHCDO has continued to hold workshops with trainers drawn from the government to develop training materials using local available resources. Further, from the initial certificate training, a significant number of teachers have now moved up to diploma level. While initially only a few primary schools had pre-schools, currently all the primary schools in Kanam A and B locations, where most HHCDO activities are concentrated, have pre-schools and the ECED teachers are now seen as part and parcel of the school fraternity. Interestingly, the HHCDO's support of the ECED centers has been so successful that the pre-schools are now better equipped than the primary schools and the project manager notes that children leaving pre-school to enter primary school have had to face some adjustments.

Challenges

The program has, however, not been without its challenges. The low wage package offered to ECED teachers has made retaining them difficult. This has been exacerbated by the fact that in some instances even the little pay they get is delayed due to late payment of fees by parents. The government, on the other hand, continues to provide only minimal support to ECED activities and the project manager observes that in the whole of the Rachuonyo district there are only three government staffers at the District Early Childhood Education Center (DECECE). This makes supervision and technical support especially challenging and has affected the quality of education offered in the ECED centers. He also notes that the government has tended to offer little in the way of support in localities where NGOs such as HHCDO exist, assuming that the NGOs will take up the responsibility of providing services.

Lessons learnt

HHCDO has over the years learnt that in order to work effectively with the government, it is important to share information and agree beforehand on mutual roles and responsibilities. Otherwise, according to the project manager, there is a tendency for the government to overload NGOs with responsibility. Additionally, it is critical to understand government policies and planning modalities. He notes, for instance, that initially HHCDO had difficulties in implementing projects with the government because it did not understand the importance of the government's financial year in determining financing of projects and therefore implementation.

Why work with the government?

Homa Hills has deliberately set out to work with the government because it believes this is important for the sustainability of the projects it implements with local communities. HHCDO sees the government as a key stakeholder in the development process and feels it cannot be left out of any development activities.

Ultimately, the project manager says, HHCDO sees the primary responsibility of providing basic services to the communities as the government's. HHCDO therefore works towards sensitizing communities about existing services offered by government as well as opportunities for improving the quality of services it offers.
(Adapted from Poverty Eradication Network (PEN) and Aga Khan Development Network (AKDN), n.d., www.akdn.org/publications/civil_society_kenya_cso.pdf)

Factors affecting NGDO-state partnerships

The case study of Homa Hills Community Development Organization and the Government of Kenya Partnership on Early Childhood Education and Development (Box 2.2) highlights very important issues which this section analyses. As discussed earlier in the chapter, the partnerships between NGOs and states, whether formal or informal, are established and operationalized within a particular context. The typologies, however, do help us understand how organizations engaged in this sort of relationship experience and observe such processes. The literature[23] is full of evidence on alternative ways in which we can understand NGDO-state relationships. For example, these commentators have, instead, analyzed factors that affect state-NGDO partnerships and highlight three major ones:

- historical and institutional contexts;
- the nature of the organizations involved; and
- the nature of the relationships.

Historical and institutional contexts

The evolution, ideology, power and capacity of both the public and private agencies can dictate the nature and quality of NGDO-state relationships. In particular, institutional and/or organizational metamorphosis may also be influenced by policies and identities. The history of society in which NGDOs operate is an equally critical factor in shaping the nature of partnerships. At the centre of this debate is how government legislation and policies, coupled with the type of regime, have such a significant influence on the nature of NGDO-state relationships. In the previous section, reference was made to Malawi's case scenario where three different regimes have had different kinds of relationships with NGOs.[24] Dr Hastings Kamuzu Banda's regime was very hostile to NGOs except those that operated on disasters and relief. In contrast, the advent of multi-party political pluralism witnessed an increased participation of NGOs both in the advocacy and broader development sectors. The enabling environment, shaped by the NGO Law, spilled over into the Mutharika regime, albeit with its own challenges and opportunities. The first half of 2011, for example, witnessed an increased condemnation between government and civil society organizations on the basis of accountability. The Nyasa Times, an online local newspaper, of 29 May 2011, carried an article titled "Mutharika Threatens to Ban NGOs." In part, the article read:

> An irate president Bingu Wa Mutharika vied off his official speech to warn nongovernmental organizations (NGOs) that supported victims of the Karonga earthquakes and floods natural disasters that he would ban their operations if they did not account for donor funds.

In his own words, the president was quoted as saying:

> "You people are always calling for government to be accountable. How about you? Government will soon find ways to force NGOs to account for donor funds they say they used to help Karonga victims. Those that will not do so will be closed. Let us see where the power is!"[25]

Not only is the president's argument above about a power struggle but it also highlights an issue that resonates with two critical development discourses of accountability and transparency. Furthermore, it depicts how easily NGO-state relationships can sour when mutuality, based on accountability, is non-existent. More importantly, it raises the question of legitimacy on the part of the NGOs which, in the case of Malawi, constantly demand government accountability (watchdog) when the NGOs have no mandate to make such demands. In reflecting on the Homa Hills case study in Kenya and Malawi, it can be deduced that government can provide a conducive environment in which NGDOs can operate only if there is cooperation and understanding between parties. Importantly, this understanding should be driven by mutuality and sharing of information, among others. These factors are not only confined to this type of partnership but also to partnerships between and among NGDOs, to which I now turn.

Partnerships between and among NGOs

When discussing partnerships between and among NGOs, attention should be given to their heterogeneity. From INGOs to grassroots organizations (GOs) or community-based organizations (CBOs), there are varied types of NGOs. For example, in some countries these NGOs are categorized into three: international NGOs, national established NGOs, and emerging NGOs.[26] Like typologies explored in the previous section on NGO-state relationships, inter-NGO partnerships have, over the years, been modeled on typologies and/or models. While NGOs have been drawn into the debate on the concept of partnerships as an expression of solidarity that goes beyond financial aid, the lack of concrete evidence of success stories on the nature of partnerships has invited further examination on the topic. In the sections that follow, I take a closer look at some of these partnerships.

Aid partnerships

Like the literature on aid, the debate on the concept of aid partnership had also attracted international commentary. Many development commentators[27] have become critical of the type of partnerships practiced in the aid industry. Research on what NGOs actually mean by partnership, how they implement this in practice, who benefits from it, and the challenges they face in developing and managing effective partnerships, remains a hotly debated topic. Various partnership models have been developed[28] but none of them is conclusive on which of these models is best suited to the development industry. The model developed by INTRAC[29] draws on three different types of partnerships based on the following:

- Funding-based difference: that is, a funding-only partnership at one end of the spectrum and a partnership based on policy dialogue without funding at the other end;
- Capacity-based difference: founded on a partner with limited capacity which requires support from the "Northern" partner, contrasted with a partnership with a strong, autonomous organization that contributes from its own experiences; and
- Trust-based difference: that is, control of a "Southern" partner at one extreme and unconditional trust at the other end.

Unlike INTRAC, Leach[30] identifies six models of collaboration between INGOs acting as donor agencies, and an ordinary development NGO.

In a *contracting model*, the INGO pays an independent NGO to provide a well-defined package for service under conditions established largely by the INGO. In a *dependent franchise model*, a formally independent NGO functions as a field office for an INGO that provides most or all of its direction and funding. Similarly, in a *spin-off NGO model*, a dependent franchise or INGO field office is expected over time to become organizationally and financially independent of the INGO.

The fourth model is called *visionary patronage*. In this model the INGO and the development NGO share a development vision and jointly agree on goals, outcome measures and reporting requirements for a program which the NGO implements and the INGO supports with funds and other resources. Closely related to a visionary patronage model is the *collaborative model* in which the INGO and NGO share decision-making power over planning and implementation of joint programs implemented by the NGO with funding and technical support from the INGO. Last, but not least, is the *mutual governance model* of collaboration. In this model the INGO and the NGO each have decision-making power, or at least substantial influence, over each other's policies and practices at both the organizational and program levels.[31] The kind of partnership model NGOs adopt may depend on three fundamental principles, which are the effectiveness of the work on both sides, the quality of their relationship and the clarity about the purpose of their partnership.

Inter-NGO partnership

Partnerships between and among NGOs vary. In some instances, they can take the form of temporary alliances, coalitions or simple platforms.[32] Some inter-NGO partnerships can be formal and legally established. One such example is NGO partnerships formed under umbrella or NGO coordinating organizations. Let us examine these from three perspectives. First, partnerships between Northern NGOs (NNGOs) and Southern NGOs (SNGOs). Second, inter-NGO partnerships from the NGO coordinating bodies. Third, partnerships arising from networks and coalitions.

Northern and Southern NGO partnerships

The discourse and dichotomy of "north"–"south" needs to be understood and unpacked as a starting point in understanding the nature of the partnerships between NGDOs in the North which, in majority, are also known as "international NGOs." The "North," in this case, represents superior, developed, industrialized nations. The "South," in contrast, represents inferior, developing and less industrialized nations. We cannot debate this issue without reflecting on the work of Brehm,[33] who studied how the partnerships between Northern and Southern NGOs have become an important aspect in the development process. However, while Southern NGOs have been drawn into the concept of partnerships as an expression of solidarity beyond financial aid, it is the practical aspects of the concept that are not only complex but also hotly contested.[34]

Too often, an inter-NGO partnership, like other partnerships in development, "is employed in ways which hide the unhealthy nature of many aid-related relationships; i.e., relationships that are unbalanced, dependency creating and based on skewed compromise."[35] This patron-client nature of partnership often results in relational disempowerment of the Southern NGOs and is usually manifested in the conditionalities imposed on the Southern NGOs. Given the multiple donors some of the Southern NGOs have, their ability to focus on their intended beneficiaries is diminished significantly as the focus shifts from their primary constituencies to their donors who impose their external development models and policies which the Southern NGOs are coerced into following.[36]

Box 2.3 Case study: Leitana Nehan Women's Development Agency (LNWDA)

Leitana Nehan Women's Development Agency (LNWDA) is a women's organization formed in 1990 amidst Bougainville conflict. The purpose, for which the organization was formed, *inter alia*, was to:

- reduce gender violence;
- work towards a non-violent Bougainville through the creation of healthy and self-sufficient communities; and
- help Bougainville women provide for and meet their own basic needs such as health care, food, education, shelter, and clothing by encouraging small income-generating projects.

In 1994, the International Women's Development Agency (IWDA) began working with LNWDA during the peak of the Bougainville conflict. The partnership was one of mutual interest. For example, in preparation for the Beijing World Conference on Women in 1995, IWDA documented women's experiences during the conflict in Bougainville to highlight the need to reduce gender violence. Three years after the conference, IWDA and LNWDA developed a joint project "Strengthening Communities of Peace." The project was funded by AusAID, the Australian aid agency. One of the purposes of Australian aid is to reduce poverty, with emphasis also on national interests. A study conducted in 2004,[1] to understand the dynamics of partnerships between local and international NGOs in a post-conflict situation highlighted issues critical to successful partnerships. The study found out that while there were elements of mutuality between the two organizations, the conditionalities imposed by AusAID had significant implications on the quality of relationships. IWDA as an intermediary organization between LNWDA and AusAID had to negotiate multiple demands of conditions which, ultimately, affected the operations of LNWDA. Under such a situation, the sustainability of projects in IWDA as well as LNWDA was affected.

Notes

1 Jonathan J. Makuwira, "Development? Freedom? Whose Development and Freedom?" *Development in Practice* 16, no. 2 (2006): 193–200.

The IWDA/LNWDA case study in Box 2.3 highlights the power of "power" through funding. International NGO relationships with their Southern counterparts leave a lot of loopholes that can easily be exploited by donors to their advantage but which, ultimately, do not help advance sustainability of development projects. Further imbalance in resources often results in what Nwamuo[37] calls "senior partners" that erode the fundamental aspect upon which the whole notion of ownership is premised. Under such conditions, the Northern NGOs tend to control and determine priorities, budgets and activities, and this ultimately interferes with the autonomy of the local institutions. In summary, the politics of aid through international NGOs raises a number of questions, especially with regard to its effectiveness and coordination, ownership, accountability, and transparency of both donor and recipient countries.

While the power imbalance is one of the many dimensions determining the partnership between the Northern and Southern NGOs, the other emerging volatile issue is what I term "implementer syndrome." Some of the Northern NGOs have moved beyond providing financial support to their counterparts and have become implementers of some local NGO constituencies. While this could prove to be a good thing, there are long- and short-term implications. For example, this scenario could result in stiff competition between local and international NGOs. In addition, the Northern NGOs may sidetrack and implement projects that have no relevance to the local needs due to lack of knowledge of the local setting. The key to this type of partnership is something that one Kenyan NGO leader observed when he pointed out: "If you want people to participate in development, you need to take them through the process of education [on development] because people can't know everything they need to know. 'Involving people' has become irrelevant. You need knowledge and then you can do a rational PRA and survey."[38] The relevance of this point lies in the power of capacity development as a form of partnership between the North and South.

Inter-NGO partnerships from NGO coordinating organizations

Korten[39] observes that one of the major challenges NGOs face in development is the problem they encounter with one another. In his words, Korten recounts that "jealousies among them are often intense, and efforts at collaboration too often break down into internecine warfare that paralyses efforts to work together towards the achievement of shared purposes. Ironically, at times, it seems easier for some to work with government than with other NGOs."[40] The scenario described by Korten above has resulted in the formation of umbrella organizations or national NGO coordinating bodies in most developing countries in order to facilitate collaboration and coordination between and among development stakeholders.

The locally mandated frameworks or government-legislated coordinating bodies are proving to be useful structures, although in some countries they are seen to interfere with NGO independence. For example, Fowler[41] has noted that coordinating bodies like the Caucus of Development NGO Network (CODE-NGO) in the Philippines, Voluntary Agencies Network in India (VANI), Tanzania NGO Council in Tanzania, and Association of Brazilian NGOs (ABNGO) in Brazil are among the vibrant bodies that facilitate partnerships among NGOs. Although this is the case, the partnerships are not immune to problems. Bennett[42] observes that such partnerships work best when they have both local and foreign support and that they do not duplicate the functions of the member NGOs unless such endeavors have been requested by the members. Bennett further maintains that the effectiveness of NGO coordinating bodies may also depend on forming other network

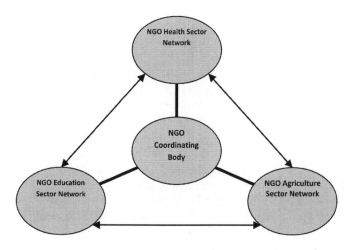

Figure 2.2 NGO coordinating bodies and their sector networks (Author's model)

structures such as a sector network. In addition, he also observes that such coordinating organizations should be endorsed by governments and society as interlocutors on issues affecting the NGO sector. How the member NGOs comply with the code of conduct, which is usually the case with NGO coordinating bodies, is an area that continues to affect NGDO effectiveness.

The "center-periphery" model of partnership as depicted by NGO coordinating bodies and their membership is, by and large, tricky. Very often the expectation is that the center will maintain and service its members in terms of coordination and information dissemination. However, this does not often occur as planned. When NGDOs organize themselves into sector networks, these networks can become very independent of the center to the point where the center becomes challenged if it attempts to be an implementer of development projects.

Coalitions and networks

Networks have become fashionable in NGO partnerships.[43] A conglomerate of NGOs may team up and form coalitions for purposes of, for example, advancing a policy reform issue. A number of United Nations summits have witnessed such networks or coalitions at work.[44] Such coalitions and networks usually operate on a common interest and agenda, with a particular theme as their focus. For example, the Association for the Development of Education in Africa (ADEA) is one coalition that works for the betterment of education in Africa and has lobbied the United Nations on issues of education.

While the three types of partnerships described above provide a broad base for understanding the dynamics of NGO interaction, there are other typologies that Fowler[45] suggests should be borne in mind when discussing inter-NGO partnerships. He identifies that the term "partner," as one of the typologies, denotes the greatest breadth of organizational interaction based on mutual support for the identity and all aspects of each organization. It is founded on the principles of holism and, as such, the partnership is comprehensive and open. Beyond the typology of "partner" comes another, "institutional supporter." Inter-NGO partnership within the framework of institutional supporter is based on the overall development, effectiveness and organizational viability of an NGO. For example, the organizations involved in this type of partnership may have a common interest in improving policy formulation, organizational strategies and operations, management procedures, sustainability and sectoral relations within their organizations.

A program supporter as a form of inter-NGO partnership focuses on a particular area of development, for example, education, health, agriculture or other sectors. The nature of support may vary, but generally it might include financial inputs, technical expertise, and facilitation of access to specialist networks. Such programs may in fact reflect the organization's strategic goals such as education. Fowler's other level of inter-NGO partnership is one that emanates from a funding point of view: "project funder." In this partnership, the focus is narrowed to negotiating discrete projects. For example, an NGO may implement programs on behalf of another institution, or at times, programs that the NGO has decided to implement as a result of its own initiative or because it has won a bid. This is different from the other level of inter-NGO partnership which Fowler calls "development ally." In this type of partnership, two or more NGOs form a coalition and pursue a development program based on mutually agreed principles, time and objectives. Whatever forms these inter-NGDO partnerships may take, there is one element that defines the success of their programs or projects: the relationships they establish with their primary beneficiaries in the communities where they work. The following section aims to analyze critically this form of partnership.

NGOs and community partnerships

NGDO relationships with local communities have to be understood through a "people-centered development" theoretical lens. People-centered development is a kind of development that emanates from below; it is conceived and determined by ordinary people in local communities. People-centered development is a social transformation and evolutionary—as such, it is a process of active engagement. Crucially, people-centered development is a process where the "participation" of each and every individual who is affected by a development project contributes in one way or the other to the decision-making process (even those that are controversial or otherwise) of their preferred future. People-centered development "enables" people to embark on a process of skills and confidence-building through collective cooperation and sharing of mutual learning.[46] People-centered development is about letting people govern the process of development in order to engender "sustainable" outcomes. It focuses on improving people's self-reliance, social justice and call for changes in social, political, economic and environmental values and practices.[47]

Facilitating a participatory people-centered development, Chambers[48] argues, is a very slow process, pointing out that there is a need to pay attention to the needs of the locals rather than those of donors who, oftentimes, are funders of development projects. Importantly, the two theorists argue that NGOs have to pay attention to the differences in the contexts within which they work, as what works in one may not necessarily work in the other. Furthermore, it is overly practical that a process of informal and personal engagement with the local people can prove to be effective in promoting NGO-local community partnerships. However, often NGOs will use nominal, instrumental or representative participation in order to provide public relations or to diffuse antagonistic protests, and as a way of legitimizing decisions made elsewhere. Therefore, effective NGO-local community partnerships can be realized where NGO programs provide feedback to the beneficiaries or where consultation between the two is not a one-sided process but stems from mutual trust.

Conclusion

In this chapter I have argued that the concept of "partnership" has become widely used in development circles with theoretically diverse meanings and contradictions in practice. Notwithstanding the complex and often unclear forms of partnerships, the current global and local development terrains are designed in such a way that the international community, composed of multilateral organizations, transnational corporations and donor governments on the one hand, and the recipient governments and local NGDOs on the other, have been brought into a default cooperation because of the need to make a difference. However, the idea of partnership, although quite rosy by the sound of it, is a discourse the theory and practice of which calls for closer scrutiny. The skewed nature of the power dynamics is, in itself, a threat to the sustainability of the NGDO sector in the South. Reference has been made in this chapter, pointing out that different models of partnerships may be applied in different contexts. No single model may work on its own but may require a suite of different models operationalized on the basis of context and need. As the case studies have highlighted, there is need for understanding of each other's motives and interests before entering into a mutually reinforcing partnerships, as these differences in interests and motives are critical not only from the point of the organizations in partnerships but also for the beneficiaries who are the constituencies of the organizations. In essence, the idea is politically laden and, in order to be able to understand the intricacies of such partnerships, one would require analytical skills and abilities. This is about the capacity to read in between the lines. Chapter 3 aims to articulate the inextricable link between partnerships and capacity building in the NGDO sector. The thrust in this chapter will be based on the belief that it is only when people's capacities are enhanced that partnerships can be operationalized optimally.

Notes

1 Alan Fowler, *Partnerships: Negotiating Relationships: A Resource for Non-Governmental Development Organisations*, INTRAC Occasional Papers No. 32 (Oxford: INTRAC, 2000); Jonathan J. Makuwira, "Civil Society Organizations (CSOs) and the Changing Nature of African Politics: The Case of the CSO–Government Relationship in Malawi," *Journal of Asian and African Studies* 46, no. 6 (2011): 615–28.
2 Fowler, *Partnerships*; David Lewis, *The Management of Non-Governmental Organisations: An Introduction* (London: Routledge, 2001); Vicky M. Brehm, "Promoting Effective North South NGO Partnerships: A Comparative Study of 10 European NGOs," INTRAC Occasional Papers No. 35 (Oxford: INTRAC, May 2001); Jonathan J. Makuwira, "Development? Freedom? Whose Development and Freedom?" *Development in Practice* 16, no. 2 (2006): 193–200; David Lewis and Nankeen Kanji, *Non-Governmental Organisations and Development* (London: Routledge, 2009); Claire McLoughlin, "Factors Affecting State-Non-Governmental Organization Relations in Service Delivery Provision: Key Themes from the Literature," *Public Administration and Development* 31, no. 4 (2011): 240–51.

3 Alan Fowler, *Striking a Balance: A Guide to Enhancing the Effectiveness of Non-Governmental Organisations in International Development* (London: Earthscan, 1997).

4 Fowler, *Partnerships*; Brehm, "Promoting Effective North South NGO Partnerships," 11.

5 Ananya M. Reed and Darryl Reed, "Partnerships for Development: Four Models of Business Involvement," *Journal of Business Ethics* 90, no. 1 (Supplementary, 2009): 3–37.

6 Robert Cox, *Production, Power and World Order* (New York: Columbia University Press 1987).

7 Lewis, *The Management of Non-Governmental Organisations*; Jennifer M. Brinkerhoff, "Donor-Funded Government–NGO Partnership for Public Service Improvement: Cases from India and Pakistan," *Voluntas: International Journal of Voluntary and Nonprofit Organizations* 14, no. 1 (2003): 105–22.

8 Shamima Ahmed and David Potter, *NGOs in International Politics* (West Hartford, Conn.: Kumarian Press Inc., 2006); Claire McLoughlin, *Contracting NGOs to Deliver Basic Services*, unpublished annotated bibliography for the Whose Public Action? NGPA ESRC research project (Birmingham: University of Birmingham, International Development Department, 2008).

9 McLoughlin, "Factors Affecting State-Non-Governmental Organization Relations in Service Delivery Provision," 240–51.

10 McLoughlin, "Factors Affecting State-Non-Governmental Organization Relations in Service Delivery Provision."

11 Ahmed and Potter, *NGOs in International Politics.*

12 Martin Barber and Cameron Bowie, "How International NGOs could do Less Harm and More Good," *Development in Practice* 18, no. 6 (2008): 748–54.

13 Barber and Bowie, "How International NGOs could do Less Harm and More Good."

14 Benjamin Gidron, Ralph Kramer and Lester Salamon, "Government and the Third Sector in Comparative Perspective: Allies or Adversaries?" in *Government and the Third Sector: Emerging Relationships in Welfare States*, ed. Benjamin Godron, Ralph Kramer and Lester Salamon (San Francisco, Calif.: Jossey-Bass Publishers, 1992).

15 Simon Maxwell and Roger Riddell, "Conditionality or Contract? Perspectives on Partnership for Development," *Journal of International Development* 10, no. 2 (1998): 257–68.

16 John Farrington and Anthony J. Bebbington, *Reluctant Partners? Nongovernmental Organisations, the State, and Sustainable Agricultural Development* (London: Routledge, 1993).

17 David Lewis, Anthony J. Bebbington, Simon P.J. Batterbury, Alpa Shah, Elizabeth Olson, Shameen M. Siddiqi and Sandra Duvall, "Practice, Power and Meaning: Frameworks for Studying Organizational Culture in Multi-Agency Rural Development," CCS International Working Paper No. 12 (2003), eprints.lse.ac.uk/29217/1/IWP12Lewis.pdf.

18 Jennifer M. Coston, "A Model and Typology of Government-NGO Relationships," *Nonprofit and Voluntary Sector Quarterly* 27, no. 3 (1998): 358–82.

19 Lester M. Salamon and K. Helmut Anheier, eds, *Defining the Nonprofit Sector: A Cross-National Analysis* (Manchester: Manchester University Press, 1996); David Hulme and Michael Edwards, "Too Close to the Powerful, Too Far from

60   *The moral case for partnerships*

the Powerless," in *NGOs, States and Donors: Too Close for Comfort* (Basingstoke: Macmillan, 1997), 275–84; Makuwira, "Development? Freedom?"
20 Andy Jones, "NGOs and the Retreat of the State," February 2008, www.e-i r.info/2008/02/29/ngos-and-the-retreat-of-the-state/.
21 Kal Raustiala, "States, NGOs, and International Environmental Institutions," *International Studies Quarterly* 41, no. 4 (1997): 724.
22 Adil Najam, "The 4 C's of Third Sector Government Relations: Cooperation, Confrontation, Complementarity, and Co-Optation," *Nonprofit Management and Leadership* 10, no. 4 (2000): 375–96.
23 Kelly Teamey and Claire McLoughlin, "Understanding the Dynamics of Relationships between Government Agencies and Non-state Providers of Basic Services: Key Issues from the Literature," *Non-Governmental Public Action Working Paper Series No. 30* (London: London School of Economics, January 2009), www2.lse.ac.uk/internationalDevelopment/research/NGPA/publications/WP30_Issues_Teamey_Web.pdf; Kelly Teamey, "Research on Relationships between Government Agencies and Non-State Providers of Basic Services: A Discussion on Methods, Theories and Typologies used and Way Forward," *Non-Governmental Public Action Working Paper Series No. 38* (January 2010), www2.lse.ac.uk/internationalDevelopment/research/NGPA/publications/WP38_Teamey_Web_final.pdf; Richard Batley and Claire McLoughlin, "Engagement with Non-State Service Providers in Fragile States: Reconciling State-building and Service Delivery," *Development Policy Review* 28, no. 2 (2010): 131–54.
24 Makuwira, "Development? Freedom?"; Makuwira, "Civil Society Organizations (CSOs) and the Changing Nature of African Politics."
25 www.nyasatimes.com/national/mutharika-threatens-to-ban-ngos.html.
26 Jonathan J. Makuwira, "Non-Governmental Organizations (NGOs) and Participatory Development in Basic Education in Malawi," *Current Issues in Comparative Education* 6, no. 2 (2004), www.tc.columbia.edu/cice/articles/jm162.htm.
27 INTRAC, *NGOs and Partnership: NGO Policy Briefing Paper No. 4 for the NGO Sector Analysis Programme* (Oxford: INTRAC, 2001); Alan Fowler, "Beyond Partnerships: Getting Real about NGO Relationships in the Aid Systems," in *NGO Management*, ed. Michael Edwards and Alan Fowler (London: Earthscan, 2002), 241–55; Helen Hughes, "Aid has Failed the Pacific," *Issue Analysis* 33, no. 7 (2003), www.cis.org.au/images/stories/issueanalysis/ia33.pdf; John D. Martinussen and Poul Engberg-Pedersen, *Aid: Understanding International Development Cooperation* (London: Zed Books, 2003); Makuwira, "Development? Freedom?"; Home Kharas and Andrew Rogerson, *Horizon 2025: Creative Destruction in the Aid Industry* (London: ODI, July 2012), www.odi.org.uk/resources/docs/7723.pdf.
28 Fowler, *Striking a Balance*; Fowler, *Partnerships*; Mark Leach, "Models of Inter-organizational Collaboration in Development," *IDR Reports* 11, no. 7 (1997): 1–13, www.worlded.org/docs/Publications/idr/pdf/11-17.pdf.
29 INTRAC, *NGOs and Partnership: NGO Policy Briefing Paper No. 4 for the NGO Sector Analysis Programme*, 3.
30 Leach, "Models of Inter-organizational Collaboration in Development."
31 Leach, "Models of Inter-organizational Collaboration in Development," 3.
32 Fowler, *Partnerships*.
33 Brehm, "Promoting Effective North South NGO Partnerships."

34 Kharas and Rogerson, *Horizon 2025*; Samuel A. Worthington and Tony Pipa, "Private Development Assistance: The Importance of International NGOs and Foundations in a New Aid Architecture," in *Catalyzing Development*, ed. Homi Kharas, Koji Makino and Woojin Jung (Washington, DC: Brookings Press, 2011).

35 Fowler, *Partnerships*, 3.

36 Warren Nyamugasira, "NGOs and Advocacy: How Well are the Poor Represented?" *Development in Practice* 8, no. 3 (1998): 297–322; Julie Hearn, "Roundtable: African NGOs: The New Comprador?" *Development and Change* 38, no. 6 (2007): 1095–110.

37 Chris Nwamuo, "Capacity Building through North-South Partnerships: The African University Sector," in *Capacity.org: Advancing the Policy and Practice of Capacity Building in International Cooperation*, Issue 6 (Leiden, 2000).

38 CDA Collaborative Learning Project, "Discuss Together, Decide Together, Work Together," The Listening Project Issue Paper (September 2008), www.cdainc. com/cdawww/pdf/issue/lp_issue_paper_discuss_together_decide_together_work _together_Pdf.pdf, 6.

39 David Korten, *Getting to the 21st Century: Voluntary Action and the Global Agenda* (West Hartford, Conn.: Kumarian Press, 1990).

40 Korten, *Getting to the 21st Century*, 130–31.

41 Fowler, *Partnerships*.

42 Jon Bennett, "Introduction," in *NGOs and Government: A Review of Current Practice for Southern and Eastern NGOs*, ed. Jon Bennett (London: INTRAC, 1997), 1–12.

43 Ben Ramalingam, *Mind the Network Gaps, ODI Research Report* (London: Overseas Development Institute, 2011).

44 Emily Perkin and Julius Court, "Networks and Policy Processes in International Development: A Literature Review," *ODI Working Paper no. 252* (August 2005) (London: Overseas Development Institute), www.odi.org.uk/ sites/odi.org.uk/files/odi-assets/publications-opinion-files/160.pdf.

45 Fowler, *Partnerships*.

46 Bill Cooke and Uma Kothari, "The Case for Participation as Tyranny," in *Participation: New Tyranny?* ed. Bill Cooke and Uma Kothari (London and New York: Zed Books, 2001), 1–15; Ian Kapoor, *The Postcolonial Politics of Development* (London and New York: Routledge, 2008); Rosalind Eyben, "Fellow Travelers in Development," *Third World Quarterly* 33, no. 8 (2012): 1405–21.

47 Andrea Cornwall, ed., *Participation Reader* (London and New York: Zed Books, 2011); Katie Willis, *Theories and Practices of Development*, 2nd edn (New York: Routledge, 2011).

48 Robert Chambers, "Participation for Development: A Good Time to be Alive. Keynote Address to ACFID Universities Linkages Conference," 28–29 November 2012, archanth.anu.edu.au/sites/default/files/Chambers%20Keynote. pdf.

3 Capacity development for NGDOs

- Unpacking the meanings of capacity building/development
- NGDOs and capacity building
- Who needs capacity?
- Conclusions

It was in 1999 in Nyanga, Zimbabwe, that I participated in a workshop on organizational development (OD) facilitated by Allan Kaplan. I was from an NGO coordinating body which, at that time, was grimacing to the ground. I think now that it may have lost its vision, and hence had no strategy. Glaringly, there was no capacity to lift the organization onto the next level given the changes in the social, political and economic landscape prevailing over the country at that time. In the process of discussing OD was the revelation that when an organization lacks capacity, it is not uncommon to notice incoherence. The organization was resource-thin. The vision was gone. As days went by it became clear that at the heart of organizational effectiveness lies the mantra of capacity development—a development discourse which, according to Gordijin,[1] Taylor and Clark,[2] and Tembo,[3] remains a generally vague concept, encompassing a multitude of approaches and methodologies and open to different interpretations and definitions. This lack of clarity to the concept at the heart of NGDO moral crusade to reduce poverty is critical to the success of their endeavors.

This chapter explores the concept of "capacity development" in more detail by deconstructing its meaning and linking it to how the NGDO sector operationalizes it in their crusade to reduce poverty. In doing so, I aim to bring to the fore the politics behind the concept and, at the same time, interrogate the tensions, contradictions and ambivalences that exist in the idea that has become popular in the development lexicon. The chapter will use the terms "capacity development" and "capacity building" interchangeably. The chapter has three main sections.

In the first section I unpack the various meanings of the term capacity, while in the second section I analyze how capacity development is undertaken in practice by NGDOs. The fundamental question of "who needs capacity?" is discussed in the third section.

Unpacking the meanings of capacity building/development

NGDOs operate in an environment of complexity. The issues they encounter in their quest to achieve a moral agenda for poverty reduction are not only challenging but equally frustrating in many respects. The fundamental theoretical perspectives espoused by many NGOs in the development field are worth exploring in order to discern the various meanings and messages relayed.

Any attempt to understand issues of capacity development should strive to deconstruct the term "capacity." For simplicity's sake, "capacity" is defined as the ability to perform, the ability to do things. One has to be careful not to think that those with a "disability" are unable to perform. Rather, conceptually, it is from this simple meaning that we are able to begin building the case for capacity development. Ronald Hope Sr[4] has aptly expanded the meaning of "capacity" in a development context. In his view, capacity is the competence of individuals, public-sector institutions, private-sector entities, civil society organizations and local communities, to engage in activities in a sustainable manner. He also points out that the form of capacity is one that permits the achievement of beneficial goals such as poverty reduction, efficient service delivery, good governance, economic growth, effectively facing the challenges of globalization, and deriving the greatest possible benefits from such trends as rapid changes in information technologies and science.

A careful examination of the definition leaves one with a desire for more elaboration. By and large, this definition is deceivingly oriented towards a modernist thinking rather than indigenous ways of being.[5] The Ministerial Council on Aboriginal and Torres Strait Islander Affairs define capacity as:

> The knowledge, ability and commitment for individuals, families and organizations to maintain their cultural identity; interact confidently and effectively with the dominant Australian society; identify goals; determine strategies to achieve goals; and, work effectively with government and the private sector to access the resources necessary to implement these strategies.[6]

One remarkable issue to note in the definition is that the competencies alluded to here are not solely confined to humans but also to institutions.

This will be expanded later in the chapter. Deborah Eade's[7] critique of the term "capacity building" is worthy of reflection. She brings to our attention the desire to seek answers to a series of questions which include: what is understood by capacity building in the context of development; how NGDOs are operationalizing the context; and how the "South" engages the "North" in capacity building. Two more questions may help us ponder over the simplistic views of capacity building: "Capacity to do what?"; and "In whose interests should capacity be built?"

The multiplicity of meanings attached to the concept of capacity building or development simply confirms the very argument that the concept is a buzzword that has gained ascendancy within the development field. Frustrating as it may be, especially when there seems to be no proper consensus on what the concept really means, any attempt to deconstruct it from an array of definitions can be confusing. However, laying ground to our main discussion helps reasonably enough to allow a critical reflection and connection to the role NGDOs play in their moral journey to reduce poverty.

From the definitions of "capacity" two key words stand out: "ability" and "competency." It follows, then, that capacity building and/or development has to do with the ways in which these traits are enhanced in order to engender the desired outcomes of a development process. A few of these definitions may help us locate the epicenter of my argument.

As pointed out earlier, many of these definitions lack depth in their articulation of indigenous knowledge about capacity building. In my earlier work,[8] I have argued that one of the challenges of development work is how certain words are used to shape people's thinking. Words can also be used to disempower people and institutions. Taken at face value the definitions highlighted above camouflage power dynamics.[9] However, there are fundamental principles that can be drawn from the various definitions of capacity building or development. These are:

- ownership of capacity building initiative;
- broad-based participation in the decision-making processes of the issues affecting ordinary beneficiaries of development interventions;
- locally driven agendas to the development of individuals, community and institutions;
- ongoing learning as the process of capacity building unfolds;
- sustainability or long-term investment;
- working in partnership with other stakeholders;
- culturally appropriate capacity development interventions; and
- trust and cooperation.[10]

Table 3.1 Capacity building metamorphosis

Term	Emergence as a development theme	Associated meaning	Focus
Institution building	1950s and 1960s	Equip developing countries with basic inventory of public-sector institutions required to manage programs of public investment	Design and functioning of individual organizations rather than broader environment or sector
Institutional strengthening/ development	1960s and 1970s	Strengthening organizations rather than establishing them	Individual organizations/institutions; also improvement of performance
Development management/ administration	1970s	Reach out and cater for the marginalized groups and communities	Delivery system of public programs and capacity of governments to reach target groups
Human resource development	1970s and 1980s	Development that focused on people rather than institutions	Importance of education, health, population
New institutionalism	1980s and 1990s	Institutional economic vitality and sustainability leading to national economic behavior	Sectoral approaches and networks, e.g. focus on government NGOs, the private sector
Capacity building/ development	Late 1980s to the present	The way to do development using other development approaches assessed against "technical cooperation"	Ownership, participation, partnership building, accountability, transparency

Source: (Charles Lusthaus, Marie-Hélène Adrien and Mark Perstinger, *Capacity Development: Definitions, Issues and Implications for Planning, Monitoring and Evaluation*, Universalia Occasional Paper No. 35 (Montreal: Universalia, September 1999), 3–4, preval.org/documentos/2034.pdf)

Morgan, Baser and Morin[11] identify core capabilities of capacity as:

- commitment and engagement;
- steady performance and accomplishment of tasks and objectives;
- partnership building and the ability to attract resources;
- responding to changes in the dynamic environments (learning and adapting); and
- managing trade-offs and dilemmas.

The idea of capacity building or development implicitly acknowledges a "gap," a deficit or a lack of something. It is an idea not only with political connotations but also hegemonic in its posture. When Harry S. Truman,[12] in his maiden speech as president of the United States, coined the phrase "underdevelopment," little did the world know what was to follow. The grand "program" of development was pushed into top gear with binaries such as "developing"–"developed," "poor"–"rich," and "Third World"–"industrialized world" quickly flooding the development terrain. "Development" took a different shape. Countries and regions considered "backwards" were soon to be "developed" through processes such as human resources development, institutional strengthening, capacity development and also empowerment. According to Brinkerhoff, capacity development was thus going to be targeted at gaps and weaknesses in the following areas:

- resources (who has what);
- skills and knowledge (who knows what);
- organization (who can manage what);
- politics and power (who can get what); and
- incentives (who wants to do what).[13]

Brinkerhoff's analysis, however, falls short of some of the current thinking in capacity development. For example, in a world dictated by those who control resources and those who receive resources, it is not difficult to notice skewed relationships. Those with the resources will usually pick and choose. This can easily affect one of the principles of capacity building—ownership.

It is fair to point out, then, that any critical examination of the idea of capacity development should be based on power, but the complexity of the debate can take a different shape and twist when issues of resource control come into play. As noted in Chapter 1, the tension often arises when the resources are provided with strings attached. This practice does more harm than good when an organization's agenda is capacity development. It is therefore critical that development NGOs possess basic knowledge of the nature of the politics of capacity development. This is knowledge about power. However, NGDOs need to be very careful; rather than focusing on "who knows what," the critical question should be "what kind of knowledge" is important in capacity development—popular or indigenous?

Another way to understand capacity development is from a "systems thinking" perspective.[14] "Systems thinking," as a set of habits or practices within a framework, is premised on the belief that the component parts of a system can best be understood in the context of relationships with each other and with other systems, rather than in isolation. This being the case, true capacity development has to be enhanced by understanding the interplay between and among different development stakeholders. This holistic approach requires knowledge. This is knowledge to do with transforming power structures. If looked at from this angle, capacity development ceases to be a process of knowledge transfer, to a model where knowledge is co-created. In this case the focus is on processes about the interrelationships between actors, structures and ideas. As such, capacity development should therefore focus on systems rather than a "capacity gap" model that denies development beneficiaries and actors the opportunity to engage in a mutual learning process where experience forms part of the interactive process that enriches our understanding of the contexts of development.

NGDOs and capacity building

NGDOs are seen as vehicles of democratization as well as providing goods and services in the Third World, where the state is perceived as lacking capacity or resources to reach the poor.[15] However, there is a catch: NGDOs, by themselves, are not resource sufficient; they heavily rely on donors. Here we need to be careful also not to blanket all NGDOs as one entity. There are international NGOs (INGOs) and those that are local. INGOs often receive funding from their governments. In turn, the majority of these INGOs often play an intermediary role of supporting local NGOs. The influence of INGOs over their local counterparts is enormously affected by the conditionalities of the Northern donors. Let me illustrate this point.

The Australian government clearly states, for example, that "[t]he fundamental purpose of Australian aid is to help people in developing countries overcome poverty. This also serves Australia's national interests by promoting stability and prosperity in our region and beyond."[16]

If by definition, capacity building is an endogenous process, the schematic presentation in Figure 3.1 goes counter to the philosophy of

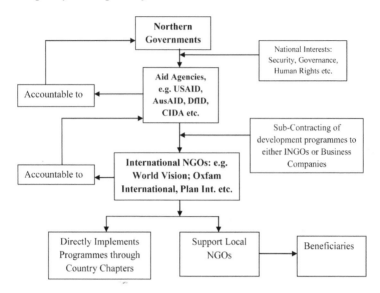

Figure 3.1 Aid architecture and administrative structure (www.ausaid.gov.an/makediff/aid-policy.cfn)

capacity development as a process that emanates from below and is owned by those who live a life of poverty. Contrary to the popular belief that NGDOs are closer to communities (true in a proximal sense), the mechanics of accountabilities are no longer "downwards"; rather, NGDOs have fallen prey to "national interests" or neoliberal agendas in the New World Order.

So the development agendas are set in London, New York, Canberra, Tokyo or Montréal. These agendas are influenced by national interests. Development is projectized, time-framed, log-framed and essentially quantified and pre-determined. The administrators of these plans have no clue of the context and the dynamics of the environment within which the project is going to be implemented. The conduits, in this case, are the NGDOs. Eade,[17] supporting her earlier observation with Williams[18] and those by Honadle and Rosengard,[19] eloquently argues that:

> Because aid agencies exist to channel resources from one part of the world to another, and because the currency of aid remains the project, despite the growing Northern NGO focus on advocacy and one-programme frameworks, it is tempting to take shortcuts in order to get things done. This leads to NGOs taking too little time

as well as the international policy context within which people, their organization and their governments are functioning. Aid agencies, particularly but not exclusively NGOs, characteristically see the aspects of people's lives that relates to their project-defined "target groups," but often fail to see the cat's cradle of shifting interrelationships in which these same people are embedded.[20]

Capacity development is a slow process, and hence cannot be rushed through a time frame compartmentalized through log frames. This is the major challenge of the NGDO contribution to the development field.

Box 3.1 One day in a class

One day I was with my class examining contemporary issues affecting Africa. As we pondered on these issues, we stumbled over the Millennium Development Goals. We then quickly zoomed into a 2011 progress report which, by and large, hinted that the sub-Saharan Africa region lags behind in many respects. The region will not meet its "targets" by 2015. One student, bravely, argued, though, that in actual fact the region has made "progress," only that it has not reached the "target." In essence, the reports seemed to suggest that there is a "failure."

While NGO work focuses on targets, it should be noted that targets are not a bad thing. After all, we all survive in our work places because we can demonstrate our productivity. However, a target as a key feature of projects, tends to encourage project administration to become mechanistic and inflexible to emerging issues. The projectization of development denies beneficiaries the processes of experimentation, learning and adaptation. Although there has been an outcry for a reflexive process of project cycle management (PMC) constantly to review planned activities, the challenge is that very often there is not enough time, resources and capacity to do all that when chasing a deadline (remember, one characteristic of a project is time boundness).

Box 3.2 Case study

In 2006, one large INGO secured funding to support its partner NGO in Southern Africa. One of the project objectives was to strengthen the capacity of local NGOs through a local network of NGOs in HIV/AIDS. Most of these local NGOs were district-based. The project document indicated that the project was to start in October 2006 through September 2009. During the end of the evaluation process, the consultant noted that:

- the project was delayed by almost one year because the intermediary INGO had to negotiate with their donor;
- the recruitment process of a local project manager was delayed due to bureaucratic procedures; and
- there was internal politics about where the local network of HIV/AIDS organizations, which was the focus of the funding, was to be stationed—at the INGO country counterpart or the National Aids Commission.

It also transpired that despite the delay, the project was not going to be extended as the donor demanded that the project come to a close. In spite of these challenges, the actual intended beneficiaries of the funding, i.e. the local district-based HIV/AIDS organizations, were hardly reached or supported in terms of infrastructure and training. Capacity development took the shape of workshops, a few training activities, but mostly it was the national office making lots of trips into the field.

The case study above highlights the inherent weaknesses of a web of interrelated structural weaknesses in the aid industry which, by inference, hugely affects the manner in which NGDOs operationalize capacity development. The bureaucracy that gravitates around financial accountability and the inherent lack of capacity to envision and anticipate the invisible challenges, creates strains that practically counter good intentions. This is consistent with Rondinelli,[21] Honadle and Rosengard,[22] Kaplan,[23] Eade and Williams,[24] Eade,[25] Makuwira,[26] and Brinkerhoff and Morgan,[27] who concur that it is one thing to make intentions known, but implementing them is a totally different ballgame. Capacity development of the poorest of the poor and those on the fringes of society, and in the case study above, the capacity of district-based local NGOs, remained elusive despite good intentions. I cannot agree more with Eade[28] that "the sad reality is that most development aid has precious little to do with building the capacities of 'the Poor' to transform their societies. Not even the best intentioned NGOs are exempt from the tendency of the development industry to ignore, misinterpret, displace, supplant, or undermine the capacities that people already have." There is no question that the way the whole idea is framed leaves a lot to be desired. It seems, though, that capacity development is for the "other" rather than "everyone" concerned in a development process. The fundamental question we perhaps need to ask is who needs capacity? I discuss this further in the next section.

Who needs capacity?

In 1998, I was privileged to have been offered a job as a research information and networking manager by the Council for NGOs in Malawi (CONGOMA), an umbrella organization for NGOs in Malawi. At this juncture, I had just made a transition, or, if you like, a career change, from education into the development field. One of my duties was to assess submissions for NGOs that wanted to be members of the council. It quickly dawned on me that almost every NGO that applied for membership had in their mission, vision or objectives, *building capacity of their beneficiaries* as the central theme. I vividly remember having a casual conversation with a colleague, jokingly saying, "one could wake up one morning, develop a proposal, set an NGO, and seek funding aimed at building people's or organizational capacities." It is quite obvious that organizations seeking membership are largely what are known as "emerging NGOs." Based on this organizational status, one wonders how, as newly established NGDOs, they would suddenly acquire skills to build the capacity of others? The answer to the question lies in the observations by Eade[29] who, in her analysis of NGOs and capacity development, made two critical conclusions. First, that while NGOs may be no worse than other development actors, they do not have any inherent capacity to build the capacities of "the poor." She further continued to argue that operational NGOs tend to replace rather than build local capacities.

In my earlier work,[30] I formulated an argument using a case study of indigenous communities in Australia, highlighted by Figure 3.2.

The analysis of capacity building is often located in the context of "us and them," which brings the whole debate into power relationships. It all starts from the very notion of "development." The perception that there is such a thing as development creates a fertile ground that supports and perpetuates "the developer"–"the developed" mentality. Kaplan[31] captures this argument, stating that when we look at capacity development from an organizational perspective, the emphasis is the "lack of," for example, resources and skills. For an organization that lacks self-reflection, this is the moment a blame game starts. In the model in Figure 3.3, capacity building is about looking at the dyna-mism created by various actors. Capacity development, in this context, is

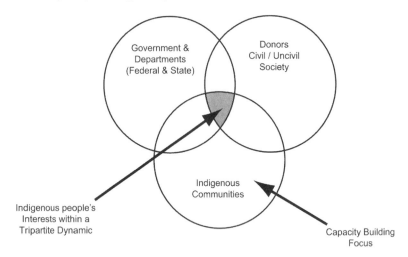

Figure 3.2 The dynamics of capacity building (Jonathan J. Makuwira, "The Politics of Community Capacity Building: Contestations, Contradictions, Tensions and Ambivalences in the Discourse in Indigenous Communities in Australia", *The Australian Journal of Indigenous Education* 36, Supplement (2007): 129–36)

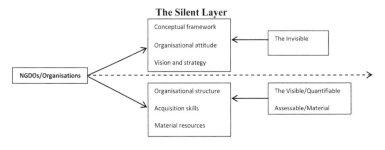

Figure 3.3 NGDO capacity-building focus (Alan Kaplan, "Capacity Building: Shifting the Paradigm of Practice," *Development in Practice* 10, nos. 3 & 4 (2000): 517–26).

not just about the poor; rather, it is about a holistic approach to the entire system within which the so-called "poor" or "powerless" find themselves. Ajulu[32] brings in new insights into the capacity development debate. She argues that while the poor, marginalized communities or organizations on the fringes of society may be viewed as powerless victims, it can also be argued that the actions of the rich, the policy makers and those in positions of influence and power perpetuate powerlessness—their helplessness to change things to improve the situation of the poor contributes to the perpetuation of poverty.[33]

Viewed from this angle, as well as given the current critique about the role of NGOs in development,[34] NGDOs may not be a panacea to the ills of development. Changes in the social, political and economic environments should provide NGDOs with an opportunity to engage in self-reflection. For example, regime change in a particular context may be enough reason for NGDOs to refocus their capacity building activities. Another good example is the current global financial crisis, the ramifications of which on NGDO funding are far reaching. How NGDOs adapt to such unprecedented events matters, as they may have to shift their programmatic attention and, ultimately, their praxis.

It was earlier argued that capacity building acknowledges a deficit. This point needs further elaboration. Seeboldt and Guijt[35] offer important advice. For people to be poor, or marginalized, is an indication of an injustice. Someone's decision may have had a negative effect on someone else. Thus, an analysis of power relationships is critical for understanding the contexts within which decisions about capacity development are made.

Box 3.3 Women's empowerment

In the late 1990s, the idea of "women's empowerment" swept across Malawi. Without clear understanding of what it meant, women's organizations swiftly moved into top gear. One report, a few years later, noted that there was an increase in divorce. The report highlighted lack of proper understanding of the cultural context in which women were marginalized, disempowered and often discriminated against. Most of interventions focused on women rather than holistically looking at both men and women.

In a situation like that described in Box 3.3, NGDOs engaged in capacity development must understand the framework of power analysis. The basic tenet is that every human being has power in them. However, when human potential is suppressed, disempowerment follows. Conducting capacity development intervention that unleashes human potential requires us to understand that "the power of the crocodile lies in the water" (an African proverb), meaning that we should first and foremost understand the context of human potential. For organizations like development NGOs, there has to be a radical departure from the conventional *modus operandi*. Let me illustrate this by a case study of a micro-finance institution (MFI) in Malawi, as described by Anton Simanowitz.[36]

> Let me give one example from a recent visit to an MFI in Malawi that illustrates my point. I visited a number of group meetings at a group-based MFI. I attended one meeting run by a poorly performing field officer. Clients were late, there were repayment problems and the group told me that one person was absent who had not paid, and after the meeting they were going to go to her house to "make sure she pays."
>
> Another group was performing well, with good attendance and smoothly running meetings. Again, one person was absent who hadn't paid. The other clients informed me that she was ill, and again they said they were going to go to her house after the meeting, but this time to "find out how she is and see if there is anything we can do to help."
>
> After the bad meeting I talked to four clients who had dropped out of the program. One of them was resting due to the timing of the agriculture season. The other three had left because of financial problems and failed businesses. All three had sold major productive assets to repay their loans (a sewing machine, an ox cart and a goat), and were worse off because of their participation in the micro-finance.
>
> When I asked the good group about whether clients left and sold assets to repay loans, they thought hard and said that yes, people left, but they did not know of a case where they had to sell assets.
>
> The difference between groups? Solidarity and a supportive response to client problems. Perhaps also reflecting the input and way of working of the field officer and the MFIs' training, operations policies and management supervision.
>
> So we have one organization with a single methodology, but with different implementation and different levels of success in terms of building client solidarity. The impacts in these two groups will be very different, let alone compared to another MFI that has a different methodology, different products and services, different management systems.
>
> MFIs do influence the impact that they have. They do this through the design of their products, services and systems, and the day-to-day management of issues such as avoiding over-indebtedness, incentivizing good client service, incentivizing outreach to poorer or excluded clients, monitoring client-staff relationships, and a host

of other day-to-day activities. Some MFIs do this better than others.

We need rigorous impact assessments that pay as much attention to the inputs as well as the results. Then we will be able to start making meaningful verdicts on significant questions about micro-finance.

The case study offers a new insight into how organizations behave, especially those in development. My analysis here is influenced by the work of Kaplan.[37] I am also indebted to John Gaventa's[38] thinking on power dynamics.

Kaplan argues for a paradigm shift in our quest for capacity building. Making reference to his previous work, he recaps that an organization, loosely defined as an "open system comprising a number of interlinking independent elements,"[39] constitutes a hierarchy of importance.

The Malawian MFI case mirrors the conceptual framework above. We have two organizations with two different management styles—one with a focus on the visible and the other on the invisible. One is premised on critical reflections and the ability to observe accurately and objectively, to listen deeply, the ability to help others overcome despair. This is what Kaplan[40] refers to as a paradigm shift from "skills training" to developing "abilities." I am therefore inclined to agree with critical thinkers in this field that our focus on quantifiable indicators in our development planning reduces the power of "the crocodile" (human beings) to materialism rather than facilitating the unleashing of human potential not only to challenge the status quo but also realize individual ability to act (power to), the ability to act together (power with), and maintaining individual and/or collective self-worth and dignity (power within).[41]

Operationalizing the "invisible" component of organizational life is a matter of critical reflection. Obviously organizations are different. Like the case in Malawi where NGOs fall into three categories— *emerging* (in operation less than three years), *established* (in operation for more than three years), and *INGOs* (those organizations with headquarters overseas)—our expectation of impact will vary due to the level of sophistication, resource base, nature of the organization (whether it is an NGO or a CBO), level of maturity/immaturity, and context. Taking a radical departure from conventional capacity building is:

[T]o consider ourselves artists of the invisible, continually having to deal with ambiguity and paradox, uncertainty, the turbulence of change, new and unique situations coming to us from out of a future which we have had little experience of as yet. This more radical response would imply that we need to develop a resource-fulness out of which we can respond, rather than being trained in past solutions, in fixed mindsets and trained behaviours which replicate particular patterns and understandings instead of freeing us to respond uniquely to unique situations.[42]

Responding uniquely to unique situations implies that we should critically examine the complex terrain in which "development" operates. I have to be forgiven here for thinking of development as a "thing." It is not. Rather, I dare say, it is how development programs are implemented. Earlier in the chapter I made reference to development as a process of power relationships. It is about resource transfer from point A to point B.

Gaventa[43] argues that the foundation of how capacity building should be is a power game from top to bottom. How do we deal, for example, with aid conditionalities that tip the balance of power between recipients (governments, INGOs, NGOs, CBOs) and donors? Obviously this may require us to make some affirmations. As long as the "supply chain" of resources from the North dictates the amount of "oxygen," suffocation may not be long when all credit is due North rather than South—which rarely happens. NGDOs are caught in this moral dilemma in their crusade as agents of social change in the Third World.

Conclusions

In coming to conclusions in this chapter, let us, for a moment, reflect on what is known as a power cube (see Figure 3.4).[44]

It has been repeatedly argued that NGDOs do not operate in a vacuum. Rather, they operate in a political space which can be closed, invited or claimed/created by citizen action, facilitated by how NGDOs engage in their capacity development. However, the contexts within which these NGDOs operate can also dictate the success or failure of development. Whether the contexts/places are local, national, or global, development initiatives may collide with the visible, hidden and/or invisible/internalized power. The critical question is how citizens can act to effect change that positively contributes to poverty reduction. The dynamism highlighted by the power cube is by no means easy.

There are various lessons that can be drawn from this chapter. Broadly, the chapter has highlighted that there is no single way to capacity development, given that NGDOs or institutions are different and operate in different contexts. There is no end to capacity building. It takes time to build and develop sustainable capacities. Fundamentally,

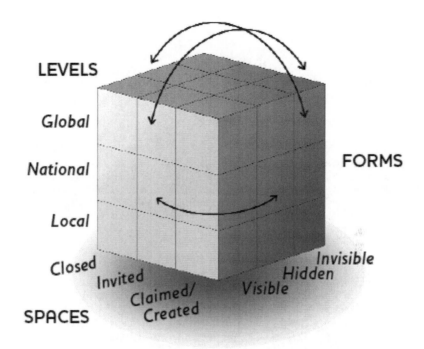

LEVELS

Global

National

Local

FORMS

Closed
Invited
Claimed/
Created

Visible
Hidden
Invisible

SPACES

Figure 3.4 The "power cube": the levels, spaces and forms of power (John Gaventa, "Finding the Spaces for Change: A Power Analysis," *IDS Bulletin* 37, no. 16 (2006): 25)

capacity building is marked by shifts in power dynamics. Capacity building is about self-reflection. Those in the field of capacity development should first and foremost strive to be reflective of their own practices before projecting others as incapacitated. This can be achieved if facilitators of the process not only foster cohesion but also encourage participants to be aware of and analyze the tensions, contradictions and ambivalences underpinning the concept and its practice. The chapter has further highlighted that good capacity development starts from where people are and should distinguish capacity building from training. Capacity building is a form of empowerment—hence, it is about having a conscience. Focus both on the visible and invisible. Part of the moral crusade in which NGDOs engage when their capacity is developed is to demonstrate that they are accountable to those they serve. An empowered NGDO and its leadership ensures that it lives by the precepts of good stewardship grounded in the worldview of accountability. Chapter 4 advances this idea and highlights various mechanisms and case studies on how NGDOs operationalize accountability in various contexts.

Notes

1 Femke Gordijn, "The 'What is' and 'How to' of Capacity Development: An Inventory Study," November 2006, www.pso.nl/documentsite.esp?docu ment=801.
2 Peter Taylor and Peter Clark, "Capacity for Change: Document Based on Outcomes of the 'Capacity Collective' Workshop," Dunford Houser, 25–27 September 2007 (January 2008), www.ids.ac.uk/files/dmfile/CAPACITYFO RACHANGE.pdf.
3 Fletcher Tembo, *Study on Capacity Development Support Initiatives and Patterns: LCDF Research and Development Phase* (London: Overseas Development Institute, 2008), www.odi.org.uk/sites/odi.org.uk/files/odi-asse ts/ publications-opinion-files/3490.pdf.
4 Kempe R. Hope Sr, "Capacity Development for Good Governance in Developing Societies: Lesson from the Field," *Development in Practice* 19, no. 1 (2009): 80.
5 Jonathan J. Makuwira, "Development? Freedom? Whose Development and Freedom?" *Development in Practice* 16, no. 2 (2006): 193–200.
6 House of Representatives Standing Committee on Aboriginal and Torres Strait Islander Affairs (HOR), *Many Ways Forward* (Canberra: House of Representatives, 2004); Commonwealth of Australia, *Overcoming Indigenous Advantage: Key Indicators 2005* (Melbourne: Commonwealth of Australia, 2005), 11.40.
7 Deborah Eade, "Capacity Building: Who Builds Whose Capacity?" *Development in Practice* 17, nos. 4 & 5 (2007): 630–39.
8 Jonathan J. Makuwira, "The Politics of Community Capacity Building: Contestations, Contradictions, Tensions and Ambivalences in the Discourse in Indigenous Communities in Australia," *The Australian Journal of Indigenous Education* 36, Supplement (2007): 129–36.
9 Arturo Escobar, *Encountering Development: The Making and Unmaking of the Third World* (Princeton, N.J.: Princeton University Press, 1995).
10 Makuwira, "The Politics of Community Capacity Building."
11 Peter J. Morgan, Heather Baser and Denyse Morin, "Developing Capacity for Managing Public Service Reform: The Tanzanian Experience," *Public Administration and Development* 30, no. 1 (2010): 27–37.
12 Harry Truman, *Inaugural Address, January 20, 1949. Documents on American Foreign Relations* (Princeton, N.J.: Princeton University Press, 1967).
13 Derick W. Brinkerhoff, "Developing Capacity in Fragile States," *Public Administration and Development* 30, no. 1 (2010): 67.
14 Bob Williams, "Thinking Systematically," *Capacity.Org* 37 (September 2009), www.capacity.org/capacity/export/sites/capacity/documents/journal-p dfs/CAP37_0809_Context_ENG.pdf.
15 Sujay Ghosh, "NGOs as Political Institutions," *Journal of Asian and African Studies* 44, no. 5 (2009): 475–95.
16 www.ausaid.gov.an/makediff/aid-policy.cfn.
17 Eade, "Capacity Building."

18 Deborah Eade and Suzanne Williams, *The Oxfam Handbook of Development and Relief, Vol. 2.* (Oxford: Oxfam, 1995).
19 George H. Honadle and Jay K. Rosengard, "Putting 'Projectized' Development in Perspective," *Administration and Development* 3, no. 4 (1983): 299–305.
20 Eade, "Capacity Building," 632–33.
21 Dennis A. Rondinelli, "Projects as Instruments of Development Administration: A Qualified Defense and Suggestions for Improvement," *Public Administration and Development* 3, no. 4 (1983): 307–27.
22 Honadle and Rosengard, "Putting 'Projectized' Development into Perspective."
23 Alan Kaplan, "Capacity Building: Shifting the Paradigm of Practice," *Development in Practice* 10, nos. 3 & 4 (2000): 517–26.
24 Eade and Williams, *The Oxfam Handbook of Development and Relief, Vol. 2.*
25 Eade, "Capacity Building."
26 Makuwira, "The Politics of Community Capacity Building."
27 Derick Brinkerhoff and Peter Morgan, "Capacity and Capacity Development: Coping with Complexity," *Public Administration and Development* 30, no. 1 (2010): 2–10.
28 Eade, "Capacity Building," 633.
29 Eade, "Capacity Building," 634.
30 Makuwira, "The Politics of Community Capacity Building."
31 Kaplan, "Capacity Building."
32 Deborah Ajulu, *Holism in Development: An African Perspective on Empowering Communities* (Monrovia, Calif.: MARC, 2001).
33 Ajulu, *Holism in Development*, 130.
34 Jan Ubels, "A Capacity Development Market? Stimulating the Provision of Local Capacity Development Support," in *Capacity Development in Practice*, ed. Jan Ubels, Naa-Aku Acquaye-Baddoo and Alan Fowler (London: Earthscan, 2010), 307–22; Daniel J. Smith, "Corruption, NGOs, and Development in Nigeria," *Third World Quarterly* 31, no. 2 (2010): 243–58.
35 Sandra Seeboldt and Irene Guijt, "The Power of Understanding Power," October 2010, www.capacity.org/capacity/opencms/en/topics/context_systems-thinking/the-power-of-understanding-power.html.
36 Anton Simanowitz, "'Interesting results … ', A Reply to Comment," January 2009, blogs.worldbank.org/psd/comment/reply/10814/594.
37 Kaplan, "Capacity Building."
38 John Gaventa, "The Power of Understanding Power," *Capacity.org* (2009), www.capacity.org/capacity/opencms/en/topics/context_systems-thinking/the-power-of-understanding-power.html.
39 Kaplan, "Capacity Building," 518.
40 Kaplan, "Capacity Building," 518.
41 John Gaventa, "Finding the Spaces for Change: A Power Analysis," *IDS Bulletin* 37, no. 16 (2006): 23–33; Seeboldt and Irene Guijt, "The Power of Understanding Power."
42 Kaplan, "Capacity Building," 524.
43 Gaventa, "Finding the Spaces for Change."
44 Gaventa, "Finding the Spaces for Change."

4   NGOs and the moral dilemma of accountability

- NGDO accountability in perspective
- Factors that have influenced the NGO accountability debate
- Competing views on the meaning of accountability
- How NGOs demonstrate accountability
- Conclusion

Nelson Mandela, while reflecting on the current development practice, said: "I have found that those who enjoy the most power and influence—even with the best of intentions—tend to over-rely on their own counsel. We see in most anti-poverty programmes, for example, a lack of account-ability by donors and NGOs to the people who are meant to benefit from them."[1] As NGDOs continue to affirm their role in the public arena, and as they navigate through the maze of moral crusade for poverty reduction, "accountability" has become the center of their practice. NGO accountability, in the words of Jordan,[2] has become one of the hot topics in the current development discourse. Because of greater visibility and influence, NGDOs have come into the real world of responsibility where "responsibility must be fulfilled, and responsibility must be seen to be fulfilled."[3] The public demand by governments, corporations, donor agencies and ordinary citizens for accountability is an expression of an acceptance that NGDOs are, and continue to be, part of the public good. Not only have they become a powerful force on multiple fronts (public service delivery and advocacy), but they have also entered a political space which, decades ago, was the sole prerogative of the state. Today, NGDOs' right to demand accountability from the state, and their willingness to respond to calls for accountability, assumes that they leverage power and power relations.[4] The fluidity of the boundaries between NGDOs, states and the markets has brought accountability into the fray as an instrument that responds to the reality that those who wield power on behalf of others should be held to account for their conduct.

This chapter aims to explore competing views on NGO accountability, especially how the discourse has been theorized and evolved over the past two decades. Furthermore, I also aim to contribute to how the concept is, or has been, operationalized in practice. The bulk of this debate will particularly center on the mechanisms NGDOs apply as rules of engagement in their quest for a moral crusade for poverty reduction. Drawing on various case studies, "accountability" as a construct is deconstructed to unpack the subtleties and, based on these competing views, new mechanisms to enhance NGO accountability are proposed.

NGDO accountability in perspective

In 2004, the Asian tsunami struck with devastating ferocity. The ripple of devastating effects was felt in almost all countries bounding the Indian Ocean. Indonesia bore the brunt. However, as is always the case when natural disasters strike, the global machinery for goodwill was set in motion. Over US$1 billion was raised or donated for the immediate reconstruction of the affected areas. NGOs, especially those in the humanitarian and relief sectors, were the primary option for rapid response. Bendell's[5] observation on the behavior of NGOs during the aftermath of the Asian tsunami testifies to the sensitivity of the accountability issue. While the reconstruction process highlighted the role and relevance of the NGO sector, it equally exposed the sector's weaknesses in terms of capacity, accountability and responsibility. Within a short time there were protests in Sri Lanka regarding malpractice in aid distribution.[6] Similar incidences were reported in Indonesia where even law enforcers (the police) were accomplices to NGO malpractice.[7]

A number of scholars and research institutions have dedicated time to study NGO corruption and malpractice.[8] Corruption scandals in emergency situations and development programs testify to a systemic challenge of a burgeoning sector. For example, *El País* of 25 April 2012, carried the headline "Six Years for ex-NGO Head who Embezzled 7.5 million euros."[9] In Tanzania, the *Tanzanian Citizen Newspaper* of 2 May 2012, also carried an article titled "Scam Claims Hit Top NGO."[10] In Nigeria, *The Daily Champion* carried this article: "Aids Committee, NGOs, and Fraud Allegations."[11] In the Netherlands, for example, journalists picked up an interesting issue in relation to a senior NGO official who earned a higher salary than the prime minister of the country.[12] All these examples and incidences scattered around the world today are emblematic of the failure of accountability at various points in a web of power relationships in the implementation of projects, programs or interventions aimed to alleviate the suffering of a particular target.[13]

When we cast our thought critically on these examples, they are not just stories that have no relevance to global politics. They are crucial in highlighting new forms of governance where the role of the state is diminished to an extent. In the context of this neoliberal agenda, for a long time now NGDOs have been seen to have replaced governments (albeit not entirely).[14] Over the years, as governments shrink and the responsibility of delivering public goods and services shifts to NGDOs, accountability, transparency, and responsibility narratives have assumed ascendancy.[15] In part, the scrutiny on NGDO accountability is not only triggered against their growth but, as alluded to earlier, their funding as well.[16]

While it is difficult to ascertain NGO funding due to the sheer diversity of NGOs, a review of the OECD-DAC (Organisation for Economic Co-operation and Development-Development Assistance Committee) literature is a good starting point. For example, 6.5 percent of the $103.5 billion of aid disbursed by the OECD in 2007 was administered by NGOs.[17] In fact, these are just estimates as other sources of funding are not included. Mayhew[18] estimates that between 15 and 20 percent of total development aid is channeled through NGOs. This new role has therefore increased NGO prominence and legitimized their new-found vision. As a result, more and more public services have been contracted out through NGDOs. It is not unusual, therefore, that the increase in the number of NGOs and subsequent funding both from donors and governments, calls for not only greater accountability, transparency and responsibility but also evidence of their impact on the beneficiaries. While this chapter does not delve into issues of impact, the section that follows discusses other factors that have influenced the NGO accountability debate, before an analysis of the meanings of accountability.

Factors that have influenced the NGO accountability debate

While the rapid growth of, and an increase in the funding to, NGOs are two critical factors that have influenced the NGO accountability debate, there are other factors that have also contributed to NGOs' increased role of accountability.

The voice of the voiceless

NGOs have, over the years, assumed the role of representing the voiceless and pushing the agenda of people power. The desire to participate in the public policy debates has given NGOs space to maximize their influence. As such, there is a general feeling that such power needs to be accompanied by accountability.[19]

In defense of political space

As alluded to earlier, NGOs do not operate in a vacuum; they operate in a political space. Therefore NGOs wield power within a political space. As long as this power is not under threat, NGOs will maintain silence. However, any threats, be it external or internal to their environment, are fiercely fought by NGOs. To justify this move NGOs have tended to establish codes of conduct, humanitarian charters and ombudsmen. A good example is the Humanitarian Accountability Project (HAP), which was initiated by a coalition of international NGOs— British Red Cross Society, CAFOD, Care International, Caritas International, DANIDA, Danish Refugee Council, International Federation of Red Cross and Red Crescent Societies, International Rescue Committee, Medair, Norwegian Refugee Council, OFADEA, OXFAM GB and World Vision International.[20]

Legitimacy issues

The conduct of governments and the business sector has raised issues of legitimacy of which NGOs have taken advantage. The collapse of Enron, for instance, and many other global conglomerates has put accountability on the global agenda. The ripple effects of the scandal in these sectors have gone far enough to encapsulate NGO sector legitimacy and called for its accountability.[21]

"Backlash" of counterattacks

The NGO sector has been given its own dose of medicine. The constant attack on and demand for accountability from companies, governments, and multilateral organizations has equally created a similar response from those on the receiving end of NGO attacks. On 6 February 2012, the then President of the Republic of Malawi Dr Bingu wa Mutharika, in his state of address on Malawi National Anti-Corruption Day, echoed sentiments that reflect this point: "The civil society sings and always pressurizes the government to be transparent and accountable ... We are now saying they too must be transparent and accountable. In fact what we are saying is that they should accept to be measured by the same yardstick by which they measure the government."[22] The scenario highlighted here resides in a complex tapestry of partnerships where mutuality is defined by a two-way accountability process. Fundamentally, it raises the question of who has the right to demand accountability, and for what purpose.[23]

Democratization

The increased discourse of democratization in the 1990s opened the way for the NGO sector to push the agenda on governments. The progress that ensued meant that one of the principles of a democratic process was, and still is, accountability. Given their advocacy position, the NGO sector has found itself equally called upon to be as transparent and accountable to those for whom they advocate.[24]

Stock-taking reports

While the NGO sector has thrived in making governments and other institutions accountable, the Global Accountability Report has found that several high-profile NGOs are far from adhering to the very gospel they preach.[25] This has heightened the level of scrutiny on the part of the NGO sector for more accountability and transparency.

Competing views on the meaning of accountability

There are differing views on the meanings of accountability. While it remains a central issue in democratic theory and practice,[26] its contestations are, by and large, a manifestation of its complexity. However, scholars such as Edwards and Hulme define accountability as "the means by which individuals and organizations report to recognized authorities and are held responsible for their actions."[27] Litovsky and MacGillivray[28] describe accountability as "civilizing power" embedded in a "relationship between power holders and those affected by their actions." Other definitions affirm similar sentiments. For instance, Fox and Brown define accountability as "the process of holding actors responsible for their actions."[29] In 2000, the *IDS Bulletin* ran a theme "accountability through participation," in which Cornwall, Lucas and Pasteur,[30] in their definition of accountability, held firm the view that accountability is not just being "held responsible" by others but also "taking responsibility" for oneself. Two issues are at the core of these definitions. First, accountability has an external dimension in which an agent, institutions or individuals are obliged to meet certain rules, regulations, standards or prescribed behavior.[31] Second, accountability is also influenced by external factors largely motivated not only by how individuals feel but also by what organizations set out to achieve.[32]

Other dimensions of accountability often ignored in many of the popular dominant debates can be discerned from Ugandan civil society organizations' reaction to a series of questions posed to them by a workshop facilitator. Accountability, to many of the participants, meant the following:

- to be answerable to those who give you the mandate: the Board and the Secretariat;
- separation of power in an organization;
- asking beneficiaries for their input and feedback;
- communicating with and receiving feedback from beneficiaries;
- responding to beneficiary needs;
- delivery of quality services in line with the goals and mission of the organization;
- downward accountability;
- making finances public;
- free flow of information;
- involvement of members and stakeholders in decision-making and planning processes;
- involvement of communities in projects;
- realizing your mission, vision and values;
- good governance;
- continually listening and learning from beneficiaries;
- regular reporting to your members; and
- accounting to the people you are affecting (*Civil Society Accountability: Principles and Practice—A toolkit for Civil Society in Uganda*).[33]

A critical analysis of these definitions highlights a number of salient issues insofar as NGO accountability is concerned. Understood from these perspectives, NGO accountability essentially entails an obligation on the part of the NGO to provide accounts to a set of legitimate authorities based on a set of prescribed rules and regulations. A more nuanced definition of accountability, which can be differentiated from a general one, is given by Slim, who argues that NGO accountability is "the process by which an NGO holds itself openly responsible for what it believes, what it does, and what it does not do in a way [that] shows it involving all concerned parties and actively responding to what it learns."[34] While all these definitions sound like very bureaucratic instrumentation of development management, we can appreciate how useful they are in highlighting the work of Najam, whose NGO accountability model identifies three distinct categories:

- NGO Accountability to patrons;
- NGO Accountability to clients; and
- NGO Accountability to themselves.[35]

Brown[36] provides slightly different models of NGO accountability. In his view, accountability models can be understood under three categories:

- principal-agent model: this is a model in which an agent acts on behalf of a principal because of an agreed contract between the two;
- representative model: in which a representative acts for voter/constituent's mandate and support; and
- mutual accountability: where parities act on and/or for shared goods supported by mutual relationships and social identities.

From whatever angle these models are looked at, a few things are clear. Where NGOs have remained donor-dependent, the accountability to patron or, in Brown's case, the principal-agent model dominates. Indeed, this view has to be accepted with careful consideration of the fact that the current debate[37] is gradually shifting to accountability downwards. This not only entails a shift in power and politics but also a clearer understanding of how power is acquired and the politics that accompanies the process to ascendancy to power. Furthermore, this process requires full understanding of the context within which NGOs work, their profile as well as other actors whose interests create contestations of power, which is often mediated through informal and political mechanisms.

The fact that NGOs have to respond to multiple accountabilities creates a challenge. While many organizations are confronted with these multiple constituencies and realities, NGOs are increasingly under constant pressure to demonstrate how, in practice, they respond to such demands. Fowler[38] observes that the extent to which NGDOs juggle the tension between many of their constituencies has often led to conflicting perspectives on how they should operate on these multiple contexts. As noted in the introductory chapter, NGDOs are value driven, but the fact that they sometimes have to dance to the tune of multiple donors results in an often compromised position where accountability is often upwards rather than downwards.[39]

At an organizational level, the challenge of accountability becomes even more complex. For example, O'Dwyer,[40] whose work supports that of Fowler,[41] observes that the challenge to NGDO accountability at an organizational level arises because of the fact that "NGDOs belong to organizational forms with no simple, widely agreed measure of organizational performance, unlike governments and business that may be evaluated respectively in terms of political support or financial returns." Organizations, indeed, are complex entities in which measures of performance are not unitary. There is no "one size fits all." This complexity leaves NGDOs open to trial-and-error kind of management which, spiced with accountability issues, makes it even more complex. So far, this section has highlighted the views and counterviews of the meanings of accountability. The critical question is: How is accountability operationalized in practice? The section that follows analyzes the practical aspects of NGDO accountability.

How NGOs demonstrate accountability

Mechanisms for accountability, in general, can take a diverse range of forms—from formal top-down processes to bottom-up strategies.[42] Other mechanisms purely focus on institutional operations with particular emphasis on capacity development, management structures, performance measurements, and accounting procedures which are often driven by legal obligations.[43] In the previous section we noted that NGOs are accountable to multiple actors: to patrons, to clients and to themselves. In the first instance (NGO-patron), the nature of accountability, also referred to as "upward accountability," the dominant practice has been, and continues to be, "spending of designated money for designated purposes."[44] Even where the money is not spent on designated purposes, oftentimes the money is spent on unrelated activities as originally planned.

In development circles, projects impact beneficiaries differently, thus opening up the whole debate about accountability downwards.[45] The third category opens up an array of controversial debate because of the complex layers of actors, both internal to the implementing organization and also those that are deployed on the ground on behalf of the organization. For example, within an organization, we have senior and mid-level decision makers and then field-level implementing staff whose actions have to be accounted for as part of the broader NGO accountability to self. On the basis of these issues, this section looks at the various mechanisms that NGDOs use to demonstrate accountability. The emphasis will be on the following tools and processes, as outlined by Ebrahim,[46] Lee,[47] Lloyd,[48] and Blagescu, las Casas and Lloyd:[49] disclosure/reports, performance assessments and evaluation, participation, self-regulation, social audits and certification systems.

Table 4.1 provides a clear summary of the differences between these NGO accountability categories as tools and processes.

Disclosure statements and reports

Disclosure statements and reports are the most widely used accountability tools among the NGO community. This is very common in any public and private sectors where those in positions of (public) service are required to provide evidence on the income and expenditure. Very often the information transcends a mere detailed account of how money is spent, to include issues pertaining to organizational structure and programs being implemented by the organization. Both in the developed and developing world, governments have set regulatory mechanisms or laws that demand the non-profit sector to provide evidence that their activities are indeed non-profit, purely charitable, or religious. While such laws exist in many parts of the world, sometimes organizations can become selective as to what information is released into the public domain. For example, in 2009 I undertook an internet search of international NGOs to find out, on their websites, availability of certain information. The variations in the nature of information available highlighted the sensitivity of accountability as a major component of development practice. Where, for example, annual reports were available, they only contained descriptive information on programmatic issues but remained silent on financial components. In others, even the

Table 4.1 NGDO accountability mechanisms

Accountability mechanism	Tool	Process
Disclosure statements/reports	✓	
Performance assessment, monitoring and evaluation	✓	
Participation		✓
Self-regulation		✓
Social audit	✓	
Certification system	✓	
Complaints and response		✓

Source: (Adapted from Alnoor Ebrahim, "Accountability in Practice: Mechanisms for NGOs," *World Development* 31, no. 5 (2003): 813–29; Julian Lee, "NGO Accountability: Rights and Responsibilities," Geneva Switzerland: Centre for Applied Studies in International Negotiations (CASIN), October 2004, www.icomfloripa.org.br/transparencia/wpcontent/uploads/2009/06/ngo_a ccountability_rights_and_responsibilities.pdf; Monica Blagescu, Lucy las Casas and Robert Lloyd, "Pathways to Accountability: A Short Guide to the GAP Framework," 2005, www.who.int/management/partnerships/accountability/Pathways AccountabilityGAPFramework.pdf)

programmatic descriptions remained silent on reflective analysis of the lessons learnt.

Earlier in the chapter I alluded to a mutual accountability case where the former president of Malawi demanded that CSOs in Malawi be equally accountable and transparent. While the principle of mutual accountability is flooding academic literature, the practicalities seem far-fetched from the reality of life. For example, some CSO leaders' reaction to the presidential pronouncements highlight the tension that exists between rhetoric and reality, on disclosure issues: "We at CHRR and CEDEP, without being pessimistic are of the view that permitting parliament to exercise that so-called 'legislative oversight' is the beginning of a process towards systematic elimination of civil society organizations which the government considers a thorn in the flesh."[50] Hardly do these sentiments provide evidence beyond doubt that without clear legislation NGOs are under no obligation to exercise transparency and accountability upwards to entities that are not part of patron-client setup. More importantly, these sentiments also raise the question of who demands accountability and why.

Participation

Participation, as an approach through which NGOs can demonstrate accountability, is a difficult process as is the meaning of the concept itself. As part of an ongoing routine in an organization that espouses rights-based approaches to development, participation must not be viewed as an outcome of a process but rather as an intrinsic thing that should be considered a fundamental right.[51] Before applying it as an approach to NGO accountability, it needs to be fully understood that participation has different and conflicting meanings. Feeney contends that "participation is a fundamental human right. It is a means of engaging poor people in joint analysis and development of priorities. Its ultimate goal should be to foster the existing capacities of local, poor women and men to increase their self-reliance in ways that outlast specific objectives. The purpose of participation is to give a voice to poor or marginalized people and integrate into the decision-making structures and processes that shape their lives."[52]

A number of issues can be discerned from the definition. First, participation as a construct is an admission of the failure of development. Second, the concept reveals that there are levels of participation that can be measured by stakeholder influence on the decision making (depth), the range of stakeholders involved (breadth), and stages of the process in which stakeholders are engaged (timing). Drawing from Cornwall's[53] model, participation occurs in a continuum which spans from being a passive participant to a transformative level where those involved influence processes and take control of events. At its basic level, NGOs can engage beneficiaries as "objects" of a development process. This level of participation is purely functional, with the aim basically to entrust people in the project or processes so that compliance is secured, dissent is suppressed and legitimacy is gained and endorsed.

Above "functional" participation is "*instrumental*" participation. NGOs can use this level of participation to engage local people as instruments of a process where beneficiaries contribute to the project through sporadic involvement in activities that NGOs may delegate. So far, project decisions are top-down.

The third of Cornwall's levels is where NGOs can use beneficiaries as "actors" and active stakeholders in the decision-making process. The process is more *consultative* and projects implemented under this category are reflective of popular views, values and ideas. However, the fundamental ingredient absent in this is ownership. Therefore, while the process may be consultative, very often it is at this stage that systematic opposition to the project is diffused and public responsiveness to the project idea is espoused. One good thing is that there is some level of negotiation.

The last or the highest order of the continuum of the levels of participation is where NGOs can use their beneficiaries as agents of change. They let go of the stick[54] and allow citizen participation which "*transforms*" political processes, allows popular dissent, accommodates difference, raises public consciousness, enables recipients to have what is rightfully theirs, and enhances accountability. Decision-making processes emanate from below. In this category, NGOs are facilitators of development processes and co-producers as well as generators of knowledge.

The widespread use of this approach to NGO accountability is not free from scrutiny. On the one hand there is the problem of upward accountability. It is also very difficult to aggregate the huge amounts of context-specific data from participatory methodologies. While highly espoused by NGOs,[55] it is observed that there are problems with the quality of participatory processes which are often dictated by the extent to which local people pledge their commitment and, also, how the NGOs value local indigenous knowledge. Where participation is predominantly functional and instrumental, Najam concedes that "the sham of participation translates into the sham of accountability" because "unlike donors, communities cannot withdraw their funding: unlike the governments, they cannot impose conditionalities."[56] In Hirschmann's terminology, "participation in the exercise of quoted voice is largely symbolic in such settings; it is not political action par excellence."[57]

If we consider participation as a form of empowerment, then the current practices of participatory approaches (PRAs) and accompanying tools, bring to the fore the flaws and weaknesses in undermining power relations. By definition, empowerment as a form of participation entails:

- increasing the power of the disadvantaged;[58]
- an indigenous process that emanates from below and is gained by principles of relationship building and participation;[59]
- ordinary people discovering their capacity to solve their own problems and controlling the means to do so;[60] and
- capability of ordinary people to negotiate with and hold institutions and those in power to account.

This means that participation is a complete transformation of power relations where those on the fringes of society assume greater responsibility, command issues, influence events and take control of development processes. In this context, participation as a process of accountability requires a complete balance of upwards and downwards accountabilities.

Before we even think of considering participation as a process of accountability, Saleebey's[61] advice is critical. He warns that: "to discover the power within people and communities, we must subvert and abjure pejorative labels; provide opportunities for connection to family, institutional, and communal services; assail the victim mindset; foreswear paternalism; trust people's intuitions, accounts, perspectives, and energies; and believe in people's dreams."[62]

Without necessarily going into the mist of this debate, the very foundation of conceiving projects in the "developed" contexts defeats the whole notion of participatory processes because what follows after is largely rubber stamping. Think of a situation where a government—for example, Australia or any other—subcontracts an organization such as ACIL, GRM or Cardno, to implement projects on its behalf. These intermediary organizations are business oriented and time conscious. One of the challenges of institutionalizing participation as an accountability process is the administrative nature of the process; the amount of resources needed to achieve optimal participation and how to accommodate differing views against a time-bound activity. Bendell observes that the process of participation has now become "industrialized with consultants so that such processes are little more than [an] exercise in gaining consent for predetermined strategies."[63] Similar sentiments are also echoed by Cooke and Kothari,[64] who point out that participatory processes to accountability have just become mere self-serving instruments.

While the discourse of participatory methodologies has gained ascendancy over the past two decades, it is now coming under constant scrutiny particularly due to its emphasis on local contexts while disregarding the global political economy of development. In concluding one of my last lectures of the semester in one of my classes where I teach the course "Aid, Adjustment and Development," I invited my students to reflect and sum up what they had learnt. One of them summed up this way: "My take is that participatory processes seem to focus on the 'victims' of development rather than the 'victimizers' of development such as the IMF [International Monetary Fund] and World Bank." This statement reminded me of Ajulu,[65] whose arguments I have often used in my writing. She argues that while the poor are powerless victims, it can also be argued that the rich, policy makers or those people in positions of power, and whose actions perpetuate powerlessness, are also *powerless* in one way or another. In this case, they can easily be identified as *powerless victors*. This is because while they do not suffer in the same way as the poor, "their powerlessness—their helplessness to change things to improve the situation of the poor, contributes to the perpetuation of poverty. The way they suffer personally, however, is in some loss of humanity."[66]

Putting all these perspectives together offers a critical examination of NGDOs as moral crusaders in their quest for poverty alleviation. Given their emphasis on projects, while at the same time employing participatory processes, one of the key and thorny issues NGDOs face is the often overinflated claims of their impact. In their new edition of *Ontrac*, INTRAC[67] notes that NGOs should focus more on long-term change rather than project-focused outputs and outcomes. By employing "theories of change" approaches, NGOs can focus on what needs to be changed rather than what needs to be done. In this case NGO accountability downwards changes from ticking boxes as is often the case with a logical framework approach, to demonstrating the contribution of projects on the broader social, political, economic and environmental issues.

Self-regulation/code of conduct

Self-regulation has become a mechanism and an emerging trend in the governance of social and economic activities, not only within the NGO community but also in other institutions in the public and private sectors of social development. Self-regulation, as used in this chapter, refs to all the efforts made by public and private entities (in our case here, NGDOs), to develop a set of rules, standards or code of conduct/ behavior or performance.[68] In the wake of an emerging sector seizing on every single opportunity for exposure as trusted conduits of donor funding, NGOs are exposed for dismal performance and a series of scandals that have tainted their image as organizations bearing the "moral high ground" slogan. The fact that different NGOs mature differently has given rise to the debate that used to be at the heart of the corporate world. Now, because of their role in society, NGOs are not only required to demonstrate impact but also account for how inputs translate into results. Lloyd affirms that "NGO self-regulation has emerged because worldwide, for reasons related to the dominance of economic globalisation and the decline of state intervention as a credible policy, states are both less able and less willing to intervene in social and economic activities."[69]

NGO self-regulation is also a product of interrelated processes. These have been highlighted in the preceding sections but, in brief, they constitute:

- rapid growth of NGOs which has increased their power and influence;
- legitimacy and representativeness;
- increased funding;
- internal governance and external accountability;
- retention of public trust and confidence; and
- proof of their effectiveness as a way of opening up other avenues for funding.[70]

Box 4.1 Case study: Australian Council for International Development

The Australian Council for International Development (ACFID) is an umbrella or peak organization for Australian NGOs. The purpose of ACFID is to "promote conditions of sustainable human development in which people are able to enjoy a full range of human rights, fulfill their needs free from poverty, and live in dignity."[1] As a membership organization, it ensures that its members are equipped with values of highest observance of ethical standards in their activities, which includes observance of the ACFID Code of Conduct.

In 1997 ACFID developed "The Code" as a voluntary, self-regulatory sector code of good practice in order to enhance and improve development outcomes and increase stakeholder trust through acts of transparency and accountability. In 2010 the code was revised and, in its current form, it sets out standards in three areas of accountability:

- program principles, with an emphasis on development aid effectiveness, human rights and partnerships;
- public engagement, with member obligations in ethical and transparent marketing, fundraising and reporting; and
- organization, with an emphasis on good governance, management, financial control, treatment of staff and volunteers, complaints handling processes and compliance with legal requirements.[2]

Notes

1 ACFID, *Code of Conduct*, October 2010, www.acfid.asn.au/code-of-conduct/files/code-of-conduct, 6.
2 From ACFID, *Code of Conduct*, October 2010, www.acfid.asn.au/code-of-conduct/files/code-of-conduct.

ACFID, like many other membership or network organizations, exhibits statements of intent which, believably, are supposed to be adhered to by their membership. However, Schweitz reminds us that while the process of developing codes of conduct and other self-regulating mechanisms is "an opportunity for self-definition by national NGO networks, as well as for public presentation of their collective mission, principles, values and methods,"[71] the sector's weakness is that there are limited or no mechanisms for enforcement both at the higher and local level. In his speech at the launch of *Inclusion Made Easy: A Quick Program Guide to Disability in Development*, held at the Christian Blind Mission (CBM) Australia, Mark Purcell, the executive director of ACFID, observed that of the 350 known codes of conduct worldwide, only a third have compliance in them.[72] In the context of development NGOs that are not confined to their country of origin, self-regulation can be a daunting task for those who are supposed to enforce compliance assessment. Take, for example, a member of ACFID whose development focus is poverty reduction in the remote areas of, say, Papua New Guinea or somewhere in Africa, or any other emergency situation. While the NGO may be bound by the code of ethics, it may be constrained by the prevailing social, economic, political and cultural factors at that moment and in that particular context.

NGO self-regulation is also important as a pre-emptive strategy to diffuse government potential to control what NGDOs do.[73] Although NGO self-regulation is good in terms of establishing operational norms and discipline, governments in many developing countries, the space and platform of which are used by NGDOs to further their aspirations, are getting weary with rhetoric. In so doing, the governments have sought to regulate NGOs. Naidoo and Lloyd[74] have questioned this practice on the basis that states do not have adequate capacity to regulate a sector so diverse and value-laden as the NGO sector. Irish and Simon[75] have also weighed in on this debate, arguing that the agenda to regulate ethics and multi-stakeholder accountability is not feasible because of the potential not only to stifle NGO creativity but also that this kind of policing may stunt NGO overall contribution, especially where governments become so heavy handed. Contributions by Ebrahim,[76] Larrabee,[77] Elone[78] and Gugerty[79] are full of stories of how governments across the globe are imposing a range of regulations on the NGO sector. A few of these examples are highlighted here:

- In the 1970s, when the Prime Minister of India, Indira Gandhi declared a State of Emergency, she instituted a law that required the tracking of all funding going to NGOs.[80]
- The governments of Uzbekistan, Turkmenistan and Kazakhstan have moved to pass laws that regulate NGO activities that relate to political influence.[81]
- In 2008 the Ethiopian government passed a "Proclamation on Societies and Charities" Bill which imposes severe penalties on individuals managing NGOs or unregistered organizations. A fine of 10,000 Birr ($800) was imposed and/or a prison sentence of up to five years.[82] The *Sudan Tribune* of 13 February 2013 carried a similar heading: "Ethiopia Bans more NGOs over 'Illegal Acts'."[83]
- In Zambia, for example, the 2009 NGO Bill mandated compulsory registration of all NGOs. For emerging NGOs or, in particular, a community-based organization, the process is prohibitively tedious and frustrating because of the many requirements which these small organizations cannot fulfill.[84]

Once NGOs are registered under such intrusive, complex and burdensome laws, the legal constraints can be prohibiting and restrictive of their freedom to execute activities according to their plans. A good example is the 2004 Zimbabwe NGO Bill which defines local NGOs as those organizations that are founded, managed and staffed by Zimbabwean nationals residing in the country. The parameters, in terms of activities, limit any foreign NGOs that engage in activities related to citizenship, community development, human and democratic rights, conflict resolution, equality, diversity, efficiency in the justice and law enforcement system. These laws, by their nature, relegate civil society organizations to service delivery and preclude their engagement with issues relevant to international conventions such as human rights.[85]

Studies by Sidel,[86] Lloyd and las Casas,[87] and Shea and Sitar[88] have developed a typology/categorization that is broadly reflected in much of the developing world. These have included, for example:

- Standards setting and performance measurement: these will include sectoral codes of conduct, self-certification, peer reviews, ratings organization evaluation.
- Enforcement and incentives: for example, by awarding high public visibility of such organizations, intranet self-regulating measures where domestic funders and their recipients uphold compliance measures, and grievance measures where people can voice their grievances against an NGO.
- Public information: through information agencies that facilitate the provision of information into the public domain with less censorship, or through charity commission or regulatory charity register, as an ongoing activity for NGO registration which can be combined with monitoring and regulation of NGO activities.

While all these initiatives are well-intentioned, the environment within which NGOs operate may dictate what style of self-regulation is adopted. No one single tool can be used and, in some cases, a combination of any of them can be applied.

The NGO accountability debate has, in many ways, polarized the development industry. In particular, the issue of government regulation through NGO laws is contentious enough for the sector. As noted above, the laws have profound implications on what NGOs do. The *Global Trends in NGO Law*, volume 3, issue 3, dedicated the whole volume to examining NGO law in sub-Saharan Africa. From registration, monitoring of NGO activities, and foreign engagement, we see layers of restrictive and intrusive practices that largely enforce authoritarian practices. Meanwhile, some commentators are of the view that government implementation of regulatory measures is, in fact, a good thing, arguing that it will benefit the sector more and it is the duty of governments to seek more NGO involvement in such resources in poverty reduction. However, Chisolm cynically observes that "there is a delicate balance between enough regulation to protect a legitimate social interest in preventing diversion of charitable assets to private pockets ... [and regulation that would] squelch the qualities that our society has most valued in the charitable sector."[89]

Box 4.2 US NGO regulation

Since 11 September 2001, new dimensions in aid financing have taken shape, with the US government very strict on NGO financing.[1] The fluidity of civil society organizations is, also, party to the challenge as certain organizations pursue different agendas which can easily be misconstrued as terrorist activities. Therefore, the US government has since introduced regulations that its funding procedures should first screen those that are listed as terrorist organizations or potential terrorist organizations.

Notes

1 Jem Bendell, "Debating NGO Accountability," 2006, www.un-ngls. org/orf/pdf/NGO_Accountability.pdf.

Where governments are regulating NGOs through intermediary organizations like national umbrella organizations, the reactions are mixed. Case studies from Kenya, Malawi and Botswana highlight this argument.[90]

In 1998, I was privileged to work for the Council for Non-Governmental Organizations in Malawi (CONGOMA). At the time of my arrival, the organization was undergoing a difficult period because of issues of maladministration related to funding. CONGOMA was an organization that emerged from the Council for Social Welfare in Malawi. As the number of NGOs increased both as a result of increased refugees settling in Malawi due to the Mozambican civil war and the changing political landscape, these NGOs needed a representative body. In 1992, CONGOMA was officially created under an act of parliament. The organization was created to promote an enabling environment for NGO activities; to foster and enhance collaboration and cooperation among members and between members and other agencies; to provide information and undertake and encourage networking activities; and to enhance institutional capacity development in its member organizations.[91]

In 1998/99 a process to develop an NGO law came into effect. Gugerty[92] notes that during the consultative phase of legislative design, CONGOMA facilitated a series of meetings between nonprofits and government officials over the content of legislation. When the provisions of the proposed NGO Act were made public in late 2000, however, the contents were a surprise to many NGOs. The Act designated CONGOMA as the official coordinating body for NGOs, required all NGOs to join the association, and charged CONGOMA with developing and maintaining a code of conduct for the sector. Some NGOs felt the Act gave the government and CONGOMA excessive powers, and 15 prominent NGOs issued a public appeal against the bill.[93] With little consensus among its members, CONGOMA's membership was fractured along ideological lines—those that supported the bill and those that were against it. Not only did this create administrative challenges but it also weakened the organization's authority.

One of the programs I witnessed grow in popularity during the period was the establishment of "sector networks." This was meant to help collaboration and information sharing among NGOs working in the same sector. While this was a good thing, these networks grew stronger and subsequently did not see the need to be monitored by the secretariat. It was apparent later in the process that the government began to notice the shift in the behavior of NGOs—that the government was losing control over the NGOs. The move to legislate the NGOs was triggered by this event. CONGOMA, in one of its reports from a series of consultative meetings, observes that:

> NGOs' view [was] that initially government regarded them as complementing its development efforts but it seems this picture is gradually being eroded. There seems to be suspicion on part of government on the role of NGOs, sometimes viewed as competing with its institutions or having political ambitions, especially those NGOs in the human rights sector. NGOs feel government should concentrate on its core regulatory roles and creation of an enabling environment within without interfering with NGO operations.[94]

Over the years, even after passing the NGO law, the NGO-government relationship is as sour as ever.[95] Lately the tension between government and CSOs in Malawi has been tense following the intention of the Mutharika administration to legislate for strict monitoring of NGO activities.[96] The reactions from the CSOs are symptomatic of the challenges of regulation as a means for enhancing accountability.

Performance assessment, monitoring and evaluation

I have consistently made reference to NGDOs' contribution and the need to provide evidence of their success. These days it is not unusual to hear of "participatory monitoring and evaluation" (PM&E). All there is in the PM&E debate is essentially accountability downwards. Broadly, monitoring and evaluation have become core elements of a development process. There are two major issues related to this: monitoring and evaluation for learning and also accountability.[97] In an era when every coin is provided to make a difference, performance assessments, monitoring and evaluation have inevitably become key elements of accountability. For effective PM&E to take place, a regular and systematic collection, analysis, interpretation and use of data is required. In any development activity, this process has two dimensions: using data to inform decisions and improve practice (learning) and, if used summatively, to demonstrate the worth of a development activity.

The functions of PM&E, for example, are taken for granted, are without proper scrutiny. The challenge for the development industry is to view monitoring as a regular collection of data while evaluation as a periodic occurrence of making sense of data. This is deceiving. The two are inextricably linked. Where monitoring stops and evaluation begins remains unclear. In fact, monitoring is a form of evaluation. Establishing a PM&E system in a development organization is therefore a critical undertaking in fulfilling one of the main reasons for it—that is, accountability. PM&E as an instrument for accountability is demonstrating to donors, development beneficiaries, and other implementing partners that inputs, expenditure, and results are "value for money" or are reasonably within planned activities. While the emphasis is upward accountability to donors, better accountability is linked to participation— where the beneficiaries become part of the monitoring and evaluation process. Enhanced learning through participatory monitoring and evaluation and regular performance assessment can potentially create a sense of collective accountability among development beneficiaries. Unfortunately, in practice, it is less so, especially when PM&E for accountability is looked at from a patron-client perspective.

Box 4.3 Australia NGO Cooperation Program

Between September 2011 and February 2012, the Australian government's development wing, AusAID and five major Australian INGOs entered into a trial project to develop a monitoring evaluation and learning framework (MELF). MELF is meant to cater for the needs of various development stakeholders, especially those funded by AusAID. Primarily, MELF was designed as a tool to ensure satisfactory and consistent monitoring and reporting by Australian NGOs funded under the

Australia NGO Cooperation Program (ANCP). Specifically, MELF's objectives are to:

- provide accountability of AusAID funding to Australian NGOs in line with the objectives of ANCP;
- provide information about overall program performance of ANCP programs highlighting areas for improvement and further development;
- provide information about the range and scope of ANCP-funded work in line with AusAID's Transparency Charter,[1] and other external audiences;
- provide information about high-level outcomes achieved through the funding provided under ANCP, including reporting against AusAID's results framework; and
- provide an opportunity to share learning about development effectiveness for both AusAID and Australian NGOs.[2]

According to the framework, the MELF aligns with the Australian government's strategic goals of saving lives, promoting opportunities for all, sustainable economic development, effective governance, and humanitarian and disaster response. The following principles underpin the MELF:

- The MELF will establish common monitoring and evaluation processes for ANCP agencies, including indicators and data sets to capture results, whilst also recognizing existing NGO monitoring, evaluation and learning systems, and utilizing information available through these systems.
- The MELF will utilize the existing quality control and aid effectiveness mechanisms (that is AusAID accreditation and ACFID Code of Conduct) to which Australian NGOs are already subject, avoiding duplication of these existing processes.
- The MELF will streamline the formal reporting requirements for both NGOs and AusAID in order to increase development effectiveness through policy and program engagement.
- In line with good quality monitoring and evaluation practice, the MELF will balance the multiple purposes with particular attention to accountability and learning to stakeholders and beneficiaries.
- The MELF will also recognise the diversity of Australian NGOs and develop a broad system of monitoring, evaluation and learning which can accommodate and value that diversity.[3]

Notes

1 For full details on AusAID's Transparency Charter see www.ausaid.
gov.au/about/pages/transparency.aspx.
2 AusAID, *AusAID NGO Cooperation Program: Monitoring, Evaluation and Learning Framework* (May 2012), 3. www.ausaid.gov.au/ngos/ancp/Documents/ancp-monit-eval-and-learning-framework.pdf.
3 AusAID, *AusAID NGO Cooperation Program*, 2–3.

The MELF architecture highlights one of the emphases placed on information gathering, analysis, reporting and dissemination as critical to the development process. However, the process takes place at meso to mega levels of social interaction. There is less emphasis on disseminating the reports to beneficiaries. While there is acknowledgment of going beyond PM&E for accountability to encapsulate "lessons learnt," the challenge the framework has is the demand placed on NGOs to demonstrate their impact through such rigorous processes which can potentially divert NGO attention to learning, to focus on ensuring that "accountability upwards" is done with the utmost accuracy.

Conclusion

The chapter set out to examine critically competing views on NGO accountability, especially how the discourse has been theorized and evolved over time by analyzing how the idea is implemented in practice. The chapter has highlighted that accountability is a means by which individuals, organizations and/or institutions report to recognized authorities and, in doing so, are held responsible for their actions. A number of factors have contributed to NGO accountability. These include but are not limited to: growth of NGOs and their prominent role in service provision; an increase in funding; NGOs seen as a voice of the voiceless; legitimacy; and the democratization of development processes. NGOs exhibit three distinct models of accountability: a) NGO accountability to patrons; b) NGO accountability to clients; and c) NGO accountability to themselves. NGDOs demonstrate accountability through such tools as: a) disclosure statements/reports; b) performance assessments, monitoring and evaluation; c) social audits; and d) certification. NGOs also demonstrate accountability through processes such as participation, self-regulation, and complaints and responses.

The discussion in this chapter has highlighted the polarity of the debate. The various NGDO accountability frameworks suggested in this chapter can only serve as pointers to a cocktail of strategies that can be tested, refined and redeployed based on the contexts within which these frameworks are used and NGOs are operating. The challenge before NGDOs and development practitioners is not just focusing on achieving accountability, but rather striking a balance between what is feasible and what is practical for the benefit of the various stakeholders in the development process.

The power dynamics have also been highlighted. While the demand for accountability is a moral call for service insofar as NGDOs are concerned, the framework within which this debate unfolds is that of a "patron-client" relationship. It follows the arguments raised in the chapter on partnerships where I explained that there are myriad challenges in the discourse of partnerships. If accountability is to demonstrate impact to donors at the expense of beneficiaries, then the efforts of "development processes" (usually rich with lessons) are wasted. Potentially, NGDOs are bound to repeat the same mistakes as they ignore the learning aspects due to the pressure to focus on accountability, yet both are equally important.

Government regulation of NGO work through various mechanisms has its own merits and pitfalls. While the process is merited on the basis of maximizing the use of scarce resources, NGDOs can be limited in many respects. The potential for NGDOs to innovate and diffuse this innovation is there. However, engaging in innovative ideas requires good leadership. Accountability and leadership are mutually reinforcing. The nature of leadership is not one where "leadership" is a position but behavior. It is through leadership as behavior that accountability can be embedded as an organizational culture. The next chapter makes a direct link between accountability and leadership.

Notes

1 Natalia Kiryttopoulou, "Strengthening Civil Society Accountability for Results: The Opportunity of Comparative Constituency Feedback," www.keystoneaccountability.org/sites/default/files/CV%20presentation%20at%20I STR%2008.pdf, 3.
2 Lisa Jordan, "Mechanisms for NGO Accountability," *Global Public Policy Institute (GPPI) Research Paper Series No. 3* (February 2005), www.gppi.net/fileadmin/gppi/Jordan_Lisa_05022005.pdf.
3 Leif Wenar, "Accountability in International Development," *Ethics and International Affairs* 20, no. 1 (2008): 5.
4 Peter Newall and Shaula Bellour, "Mapping Accountability: Origins, Contexts and Implications for Development," *IDS Working Paper 168* (October 2002), www.ids.ac.uk/files/Wp168.pdf.
5 Jem Bendell, "Debating NGO Accountability," 2006, www.un-ngls.org/orf/pdf/NGO_Accountability.pdf.

6 Agence France Presse, "Sri Lanka Tsunami Survivors Protest Corrupt Aid Distribution," *Agence France Presse*, February 2005.

7 Deutsche Presse-Agentur, "Indonesia Arrests Anti-corruption Activist for Stealing Tsunami Aid," Deutsche Presse-Agentur, 27 January 2005, www.freerepublic.com/focus/f-news/1329708/posts.

8 Michael Kramer, "Corruption and Fraud in International Aid Projects," *U4 Brief* 4 (2007), www.cmi.no/publications/file/2752-corruption-and-fraud-in-international-aid-projects.pdf; Marijana Trivunovic, Jesper Johnsøn and Harald Mathisen, "Developing and NGO Corruption Risk Management System: Consideration for Donors," *CMI U4* no. 2011 (2009), www.dochas.ie/Shared/Files/4/Developing_an_NGO_corruption_risk_management_syste m[1].pdf; Marijana Trivunovic, "Counting NGO Corruption: Rethinking the Conventional Approaches," *CMI U4* 3 (2011), www.u4.no/publications/countering-ngo-corruption-rethinking-the-conventional-approaches/.

9 "Six Years for Ex-NGO Head who Embezzled 7.5 million euros," *El País*, Bilbao, 25 April 2012, elpais.com/elpais/2012/04/25/inenglish/1335380847_1 82977.html.

10 The Citizen Reporter, "Scam Claims Hit Top NGO," *The Citizen*, 2 May 2012, www.kenyacentral.com/news/30133-scam-claims-hit-top-ngo.html.

11 Daily Champion, "Aids Committee, NGOs, and Fraud Allegations," *Daily Champion*, 6 July 2011, allafrica.com/stories/201107061023.html.

12 Jordan, "Mechanisms for NGO Accountability."

13 Shantayanan Devarajan, Stuti Khemani and Michael Walton, "Civil Society, Public Action and Accountability in Africa," July 2010, wwwwds.worldbank.org/servlet/WDSContentServer/WDSP/IB/2011/07/25/000158349 _20110725162228/Rendered/PDF/WPS5733.pdf.

14 Diana Mitlin and Sam Hickey, "Reclaiming Development? NGOs and the Challenge of Alternatives," *World Development* 35, no. 10 (2007): 1699–720.

15 Glen W. Wright, "NGOs and Western Hegemony: Causes for Concern and Ideas for Change," *Development in Practice* 22, no. 1 (2012): 123–34.

16 Julian Lee, *NGO Accountability: Rights and Responsibilities* (Geneva Switzerland: Centre for Applied Studies in International Negotiations (CASIN), October 2004), www.icomfloripa.org.br/transparencia/wpcontent/uploads/2009/06/ngo_accountability_rights_and_responsibilities.pdf.

17 Wright, "NGOs and Western Hegemony."

18 Susanna H. Mayhew, "Hegemony, Politics and Ideology: The Role of Legislation in NGO Government Relations in Asia," *Journal of Development Studies* 41, no. 5 (2005): 727–58.

19 Lee, *NGO Accountability.*

20 www.hapinternational.org/en.

21 David L. Brown, "A Framework for Strengthening NGO Accountability," Presentation to the Asia Pacific Philanthropy Consortium (September, 2003), asianphilanthropy.org/APPC/APPC-conference-2003/Strengthening-Accountability-dbrown.pdf.

22 Lameck Masina, "Malawi's President Calls for NGOs to Be More Transparent," Voice of America (February, 2012), www.voanews.com/content/malawis-president-calls-for-ngos-to-be-more-transparent-138777259/151652.html.

23 Jordan, "Mechanisms for NGO Accountability"; Alnoor Ebrahim, "Accountability in Practice: Mechanisms for NGOs," *World Development* 31, no. 5 (2003): 813–29.

24 Hans Antlöv, Rustan Ibrahim and Peter van Tuijl, "NGO Governance and Accountability in Indonesia: Challenges in a Newly Democratizing Country," in *NGO Accountability: Politics, Principles and Innovations*, ed. Lisa Jordan and Peter van Tuijl (London: Earthscan, 2006), 147–66.
25 Hetty Kovach, Caroline Neligan and Simon Burali, *Power Without Accountability? The Global Accountability Report 1* (2003), www.oneworldt rust.org/htmlGAP/report.
26 Noore A. Siddiquee and Md Gofran Faroqi, "Holding the Giants to Account? Constraints on NGO Accountability in Bangladesh," *Asian Journal of Political Science* 17, no. 3 (2009): 243–64.
27 Michael Edwards and David Hulme, "Too Close for Comfort? The Impact of Official Aid on Nongovernmental Organizations," *World Development* 24, no. 6 (1996): 967.
28 Alejandro Litovsky and Alex MacGillivray, *Development as Accountability: Accountability Innovators in Action* (London: Accountability, 2007), www. accountability.org/images/content/0/6/066/AccountAbility%20-%20A21%20 Development%20as%20Accountability.pdf, 17.
29 Jonathan A. Fox and David L. Brown, eds, *The Struggle for Accountability: The World Bank, NGOs, and Grassroots Movements* (Cambridge, Mass.: MIT Press, 1998), 12.
30 Andrea Cornwall, Henry Lucas and Kath Pasteur, "Introduction: Accountability through Participation: Developing Workable Partnership Models in the Health Sector," *IDS Bulletin* 31, no. 1 (2000): 3.
31 Ebrahim, "Accountability in Practice"; Laura B. Chisolm, "Accountability of Nonprofit Organizations and those who Control them: The Legal Framework," *Nonprofit Management and Leadership* 6, no. 2 (1995): 141–56.
32 Ronald E. Fry, "Accountability in Organizational Life: Problem or Opportunity for Non-profits?" *Nonprofit Management and Leadership* 6, no. 2 (1995): 181–95.
33 Commonwealth Foundation, *Civil Society Accountability: Principles and Practice—A Toolkit for Civil Society in Uganda* (London: Commonwealth Foundation, 2009).
34 Hugo Slim, *By What Authority? The Legitimacy and Accountability of Non-Governmental Organizations* (Geneva: International Council on Human Rights Policy, 2002), www.gdrc.org/ngo/accountability/by-what-authority. html#_ftnref11; Paul Ronalds, *The Change Imperative: Creating the Next Generation NGO* (Sterling, VA.: Kumarian Press, 2010).
35 Adil Najam, "NGO Accountability: A Conceptual Framework," *Development Policy Review* 14, no. 4 (1996): 341.
36 Brown, "A Framework for Strengthening NGO Accountability."
37 Noore A. Siddiquee and Md Gofran Faroqi, "Holding the Giants to Account?"; Shantayanan Devarajan, Stut Khemani and Michael Walton, "Civil Society, Public Action and Accountability in Africa," Policy Research Working Paper, No. WPS 5733 (July 2011), wwwwds.worldbank. org/servlet/WDSContentServer/WDSP/IB/2011/07/25/000158349_20110725 162228/Rendered/PDF/WPS5733.pdf.
38 Alan Fowler, "Demonstrating NGO Performance: Problems and Possibilities," *Development in Practice* 6, no. 1 (1996): 58–65.
39 Jonathan J. Makuwira, "Development? Freedom? Whose Development and Freedom?" *Development in Practice* 16, no. 2 (2006): 193–200.

40 Brendan O'Dwyer, "The Nature of NGO Accountability: Motives, Mechanisms and Practices," in *Sustainability Accounting and Accountability*, ed. Jeffrey Unerman, John Bebbington and Brendan O'Dwyer (London: Routledge, 2007), 289.

41 Fowler, "Demonstrating NGO Performance: Problems and Possibilities."

42 Peter Newall and Shaula Bellour, "Mapping Accountability: Origins, Contexts and Implications for Development," *IDS Working Paper 168* (October 2002), www.ids.ac.uk/files/Wp168.pdf.

43 Collin Ball and Leith L. Dunn, *Non-Government Organisations: Guidelines for Good Policy and Practice* (London: The Commonwealth Foundation, 1996), 18–20; Jordan, "Mechanisms for NGO Accountability."

44 Najam, "NGO Accountability," 342.

45 Michael Edwards and David Hulme, *Beyond the Magic Bullet: NGO Performance and Accountability in the Post-cold War World* (West Hartford, Conn.: Kumarian Press, 1996), 354.

46 Ebrahim, "Accountability in Practice."

47 Lee, *NGO Accountability*.

48 Robert Lloyd, "The Role of NGO Self-Regulation in Increasing Stakeholder Accountability," July 2005, www.oneworldtrust.org.

49 Monica Blagescu, Lucy las Casas and Robert Lloyd, "Pathways to Accountability: A Short Guide to the GAP Framework," 2005, www.who.int/management/partnerships/accountability/PathwaysAccountabilityGAPFramework.pdf.

50 Silvia Banda, "Government to Start Auditing NGOs from 2006," March 2012, www.malawivoice.com/2012/03/13/government-to-start-auditing-ngos-from-2006-2006/.

51 Patricia Feeney, *Accountable Aid: Local Participation in Major Projects* (Oxford: Oxfam Publications, 1998).

52 Feeney, *Accountable Aid*, 2.

53 Andrea Cornwall, ed., *Participation Reader* (London and New York: Zed Books, 2011).

54 Robert Chambers, *Rural Development: Putting the Last First* (London: Longman, 1983).

55 Bendell, "Debating NGO Accountability."

56 Najam, "NGO Accountability," 39–353.

57 Albert O. Hirschman, *Exit, Voice, and Loyalty: Responses to Decline in Firms, Organizations and States* (Cambridge, Mass.: Harvard University Press, 1970), 16.

58 Jim Ife, *Community Development: Community-based Alternatives in an Age of Globalization* (Frenchs Forest, NSW: Longmans, 2002), 3.

59 John Friedmann, *Empowerment: The Politics of Alternative Development* (Cambridge: Blackwell, 1992).

60 Herbert J. Rubin and Irene S. Rubin, *Community Organizing and Development*, 3rd edn (Boston, Mass.: Allyn & Bacon, 2001).

61 Dennis Saleebey, "Introduction: Power in the People," in *The Strengths Perspective in Social Work Practice*, ed. Dennis Saleebey, 3rd edn (Boston, Mass.: Allyn and Bacon, 2002), 1–22.

62 Saleebey, "Introduction," 9.

63 Bendell, "Debating NGO Accountability," 20.

64 Bill Cooke and Uma Kothari, "The Case for Participation as Tyranny," in *Participation: New Tyranny?* ed. Bill Cooke and Uma Kothari (London and New York: Zed Books, 2001), 1–15.

65 Deborah Ajulu, *Holism in Development: An African Perspective on Empowering Communities* (Monrovia, Calif.: MARC, 2001).

66 Ajulu, *Holism in Development*, 130.

67 INTRAC, "Theory of Change," *Ontrac* 51 (May 2012), www.intrac.org/data/files/resources/741/ONTRAC-51-Theory-of-Change.pdf.

68 Ebrahim, "Accountability in Practice"; Nick Leader, "Codes of Conduct: Who Needs Them?" *RRN Newsletter* (March 1999), www.icva.ch/doc00004273.pdf.

69 Lloyd, "The Role of NGO Self-Regulation in Increasing Stakeholder Accountability," 5.

70 Lloyd, "The Role of NGO Self-Regulation in Increasing Stakeholder Accountability," 5–6.

71 Martha L. Schweitz, "NGO Network Codes of Conduct: Accountability, Principles, and Voice," Paper Presented to the International Studies Association Annual Convention, Chicago, Ill. (February 2001), 2

72 Mark Purcell, "Opening Speech to the Launch of *Inclusion Made Easy: A Quick Program Guide to Disability in Development*," held at Christian Blind Mission (CBM) Australia, 2012.

73 Kumi Naidoo, "An Overview of Some of the Factors Driving the Development of Self-regulation Frameworks for the NGO Community Across the World," Prepared for the NGO Self-Regulation Workshops in Pakistan from 8–12 August 2000, www.gdrc.org/ngo/credibility/NGO-self-regulation.doc.

74 Lloyd, "The Role of NGO Self-Regulation in Increasing Stakeholder Accountability."

75 Leon Irish and Karla Simon, "The Nongovernmental Organizations Act 2002, for the United Republic of Tanzania; Gazetted in the Official Gazette 4 October 2002; comments by Leon Irish and Karla Simon," *International Journal of Civil Society Law* 1, no. 1 (2003): 70–72.

76 Ebrahim, "Accountability in Practice: Mechanisms for NGOs."

77 Stephen J. Larrabee, "Restrictive Proposals in Kazakhstan," *The International Journal of Not-for-Profit Law* 7, no. 3 (2005), www.icnl.org/research/journal/vol7iss3/art_2.htm.

78 Jeanne Elone, "Backlash Against Democracy: The Regulation of Civil Society in Africa," *Democracy and Society* 7, no. 2 (2010): 13–16.

79 Mary K. Gugerty, "The Emergence of Non-Profit Self-regulation in Africa," *Nonprofit and Voluntary Sector Quarterly* 39, no. 6 (2010): 1087–112.

80 Ebrahim, "Accountability in Practice: Mechanisms for NGOs."

81 Larrabee, "Restrictive Proposals in Kazakhstan."

82 Elone, "Backlash Against Democracy."

83 allafrica.com/stories/201302220066.html.

84 Mandeep S. Tiwana, "Analysis of the Restrictive Aspects of the Ugandan NGO Registration Act, 1989, the NGO Registration (Amendment) Act, 2006 and the NGO Regulations, 1990," *Civil Society Watch*, CIVICUS (2008), www.civicus.org/content/Analysis-Uganda-NGO-legal-framework.pdf.

85 Elone, "Backlash Against Democracy."

86 Mark Sidel, *Trends in Non-profit Self-Regulation in the Asia Pacific Region: Initial Data on Initiatives, Experiments and Models in Seventeen Countries* (University of Iowa, 2003).

87 Robert Lloyd and Lucy de las Casas, *NGO Self-Regulation: Enforcing and Balancing Accountability* (London: OneWorld Trust, 2005), www.oecd.org/dev/devcom/44251309.pdf.

88 Catherine Shea and Sandra Sitar, *NGO Accreditation: The Way Forward? An Evaluation of the Development Community's Experience—Report and Recommendations* (Washington, DC: International Center for Not for Profit Law, n.d.), pdf.usaid.gov/pdf_docs/PNADB766.pdf.

89 Chisolm, "Accountability of Nonprofit Organizations and those who Control them," 149.

90 Gugerty, "The Emergence of Non-Profit Self-regulation in Africa."

91 Jonathan J. Makuwira, "The NGO Law in Malawi," Paper Presented at the Policy Advocacy Conference for NGO Leaders in Malawi (Mangochi: Club Makokola, 1998).

92 Gugerty, "The Emergence of Non-Profit Self-regulation in Africa."

93 Heiko Meinhardt and Nandini Patel, *Malawi's Process of Democratic Transition: An Analysis of Political Developments Between 1990 and 2003* (Sankt Augustin, Germany: Konrad Adenauer Foundation, 2003); Gugerty, "The Emergence of Non-Profit Self-regulation in Africa," 1100.

94 Council for NGOs in Malawi (CONGOMA), *Consultative Appraisal: Final Report*, 2001, web.onetel.com/~fanwellbokosi/docs/congoma.pdf, 9.

95 Jonathan J. Makuwira, "Civil Society Organizations (CSOs) and the Changing Nature of African Politics: The Case of the CSO–Government Relationship in Malawi," *Journal of Asian and African Studies* 46, no. 6 (2011): 615–28.

96 *Malawi Voice*, "CSO's Reaction to Bingu's Speech on the Opening of Parliament," 2012, www.malawivoice.com/2012/02/14/csos-reaction-bingus-speech-on-the-opening-of-parliament/.

97 Patricia J. Rogers and Bob Williams, "Evaluation for Practice Improvement and Organizational Learning," in *Handbook of Evaluation*, ed. Ian F. Shaw, Jennifer C. Greene and Melvin M. Mark (London: Sage Publications, 2006), 76–97.

5   NGO leadership and management

- Leadership and management in context
- Leadership, management and governance in development
- Leadership theories and change in development
- Organizational growth and leadership challenges
- Leaderful leadership and development
- Servant leadership in development NGOs
- Conclusion

In a complex world of development, nothing is more important than visionary leadership. In institutions like NGDOs, both good leadership and management are critical. Development organizations that are well managed are fundamental building blocks for the promotion of change. In saying so, it needs to be acknowledged that leading people to perform their duties efficiently and effectively is a big challenge. For today's development organizations, there is a great need for effective leaders who understand the complexities of the ever-changing social, political, economic, and ecological environments and are able to adapt constantly to new and unpredictable environments and, at the same time, adopt new technologies. The NDGOs sector needs leaders who have the intelligence, sensitivity and ability to empathize with others and those that can motivate their workmates around them to strive for success. The challenge for the development sector in the twenty-first century is not just being at the helm of an organization, but also to recognize the opportunity that exists between themselves and the grassroots communities. Essentially, it means to prove with evidence, the success, the change, and the impact an organization makes in a community. For that to happen, the ingredients transcend personalities. It goes beyond having skills. It requires people with abilities. These are leaders who are defined by their behavior. As Newman[1] once said, today's leaders should be long-term thinkers who see beyond the day's crisis and the quarterly report.

In this chapter I aim to examine critically the importance of leadership in development organizations. In canvassing this concept, I shall discuss management and governance issues in relation to development projects. The chapter starts with an examination of the idea of leadership before discussing the differences between leadership, management and governance. The third section of the chapter deals with leadership theory and change in a development context and further highlights the importance of organizational growth and leadership challenges. The last two sections of the chapter posit an argument that conventional leadership theories as "being out in front" are no longer viable in development organizations driven by moral values. Rather, today's development organizations should strive to establish communities with a leadership fundamentally driven by the desire for service, not sequentially but concurrently and collectively.[2]

Leadership and management in context

Defining leadership and management within a development context is a challenging task. I have argued earlier that development is context-specific. This is equally true with the meanings of leadership. No one definition captures the nuances of both leadership and management. As development practitioners, we must be open to exploring various meanings of both concepts from the perception of the NGO world. Yukl[3] acknowledges the controversy that exists on the difference between leadership and management. The challenge that underpins the debate emanates from the questions on whether a person can be a leader without being a manager or, vice versa. The elusiveness of the answer to this question not only shows how polarized the debate on these themes is, but also shows that in the context of the NGO sector we need to pay careful attention to the contradictions and tension each of these concepts raises and, ultimately, find the creative balance.[4]

Despite this complexity some scholars have argued that leadership and management are qualitatively different and mutually exclusive.[5] The challenge embedded in many of the assumptions is that leadership and management cannot occur in the same person. In some cases it may even be extrapolated that leadership and management values are incompatible and depict different personalities. Yet, while many of the definitions of leadership and management are from the corporate world, their applicability to the NDGO sector cannot be overemphasized. Kaplan[6] observes that while leadership and management may not mean the same thing, there is, however, interconnectedness between them.

One of the classic differences between leaders and managers, according to Bennis and Nanus, is that "managers are people who do things right, and leaders are people who do the right things."[7] That said, however, examining a few definitions of leadership and management may help us to draw out some principles that may underpin our work. Let me emphasize one point: leadership is a social and cultural phenomenon. A leader or manager who is considered effective in Australia may be considered an authoritarian in New Zealand. A leader or manager in Oxfam Canada may not be effective in leading/managing Plan International in Cambodia. Therefore, understanding leadership or management requires us to understand the cultural context in which these concepts take place. According to Kotter,[8] the importance of leadership and managing is, in part, dependent on the situation. In the context of NGOs, as they become larger due to scaling up of their activities, managing may become a necessary component. In a similar vein, when the external environment becomes more unpredictable and dynamic, leadership may also increase. What exactly do we mean by leadership, management and governance in development? The answer to this question is the focus of the next section.

Leadership, management, and governance in development

Before canvassing the various perspectives of leadership, management and governance, we need first to understand who a leader is. Two aspects define a leader: *command* and *influence*. Obviously there could be many other traits. In her book *The Art and Science of Leadership*, Nahavandi defines a leader as "any person who influences individuals and groups within an organization, helps them in the establishment of goals, and guides them towards the achievement of those goals, thereby allowing them to be effective."[9] Here we can notice other traits of a leader. A leader "guides" and "develops." Importantly, a leader "knows."

Leadership

Based on the perspectives above, leadership is a process. It is an art. Of particular importance is the fact that leadership occurs in a group context.[10] Therefore, leadership can be summed up as a process of deliberately exerting influence within a group to move it towards goals of beneficial importance that ultimately fulfil the group's real needs. Bob Biehl sums up leadership as:

- knowing what to do next;
- knowing why it is important; and
- knowing how to bring appropriate resources to bear on the need at hand.[11]

Raelin[12] asserts that there are four critical processes that are mobilized by leadership: setting the mission, actualizing the goals, sustaining commitment and adaptability to change (see Figure 5.1).

Management

In its simplest form, management refers to the exercise of executive, administrative and often supervisory roles of a group or organization. Therefore the term "management" according to Yukl,[13] is simply an occupational title because, based on the definition above, and that of Rost,[14] managers exercise authority. Inevitably, a critical examination of the meanings of leadership and management leaves us with an appreciation of the overlap that exists between the two. When managers are involved in executing their duties, they are operating under

Figure 5.1 Four critical processes of leadership (Reproduced courtesy of Joseph A. Raelin, *Creating Leaderful Organizations: How to Bring Out Leadership in Everyone* (San Francisco, Calif.: Berrett-Koehler, 2003), 20.1)

leadership. Similarly, when leaders are involved in any aspects of influence, planning, organizing or inspiring, they are essentially operating under management.[15]

When an organization, in our case an NGDO, has finally established its vision and, perhaps, working ethics, the next big question we ought to ask is how tasks are accomplished. The next set of questions may be those that ask about methods, procedures, and policies on how to accomplish the task; or those that are to do with human resources, timelines, and exact places where these will be done. In summary the distinguishing features of leadership and management are highlighted in Table 5.1.

Governance

Governance has, over the past two decades, entered center stage of both development and political discourses.[16] Ross Garland[17] in his article "Developing a Project Governance Framework" highlights the importance of (project) governance as one of the most important factors for project success. While it is easy to define "project governance," "governance" as a concept is problematic. If we take the *Oxford English Dictionary*, the word "governance" is understood as "action or

Table 5.1 Differences between leaders and managers

Subject	Leader	Manager
Essence	Change	Stability
Focus	Leading people	Managing work
Have	Followers	Subordinates
Horizon	Long term	Short term
Seeks	Vision	Objectives
Approach	Sets direction	Plans detail
Decision	Facilitates	Makes
Power	Personal	Formal authority
Appeal to	Heart	Head
Energy	Passion	Control
Dynamic	Proactive	Reactive
Persuasion	Sell	Tell
Rules	Breaks	Makes
Likes	Striving	Action
Risks	Takes	Minimizes
Conflict	Uses	Avoids
Direction	New roads	Existing roads
Credit	Gives	Takes
Blame	Takes	Blames

Source: (www.vatl.org.au)

manner of governing"; "to rule with authority"; "to direct and control actions and affairs of (people, a state or its members)"; "to rule or regulate"; "command." Our interest in this chapter is to understand governance from an NGDO perspective. Renz's framework of governance is useful for our discussion. Based on various perspectives, he formulates governance (at least from a non-profit sector) as "a system by which non-profit organizations are strategically directed, integratively managed and holistically controlled in an entrepreneurial and ethically reflected way, and in a manner appropriate to each particular context."[18]

The definition provides us with some clue on what governance entails in an institutional setting. Understood as defined, NGDOs are entities that are controlled and directed by the board of directors or, as differently known, board of trustees. These people protect the organization's assets and ensure the organization is functioning towards achieving the mission. Again, broadly speaking, the overlap with the concept of management is visibly apparent, with little difference based on administrative versus operational structures.

While the definitions sound very explicit about the expectations, it is often the challenge of real life experiences that test those in positions of influence to act decisively or otherwise. From an NDGO perspective, and especially those that are highly dependent on donor aid, leadership can be a test of not only being resourceful but, on the one hand, a process of juggling between creating and sustaining relationships as a resource and, on the other, maintaining a shared vision within an organization. Fowler was correct when he suggested: "It seems to me that this is the moment in NDGO history when leaders have to [be ...] motivators charting future directions for development and then mobilizing followers to generate vision of the future they want beyond aid."[19]

If indeed NDGO leaders and followers are co-creators of organizational vision, it can be argued that leadership does not have to come from the leaders. Similarly it does not have to come from the headquarters (for the case of historical NDGOs). Leadership viewed from this lens is a shared responsibility at multiple levels of an organization. There is no doubt, therefore, that in developmental context, good judgment is required at every single level. The critical aspect of this debate, though, is when we consider NDGOs in the service delivery process, and particularly those that purport to work with grassroots organizations and employing rights-based approaches. This complex development terrain challenges the orthodoxy of leadership theory and throws us into a deeper level of thinking about leadership where the line between the duty bearers (the service provider) and the "rights holder" (the beneficiaries/communities) have to be merged in order to share the vision.

In practical terms this may sound easier said than done. However, the principle remains that "No longer can one person or even a small team stay aware of the complexities of their total operation. Leaders are needed everywhere."[20] It seems to me, therefore, that the hierarchical organizational structure—the top-down arrangements—are no longer in fashion if an organization believes in pursuing a shared vision in the development process.

We need to be careful, though, that we do not locate our thinking and acts into a framework where leadership is just goal orientated.[21] Taking this kind of thinking, despite being visionary, can easily lead to short-term results. Rather, good leadership in the NDGO sector, as it would be in other sectors too, is to think about how to "humanize" an organization. Kouzes's argument is that leading at a higher level eventually means engaging in a process whereby one pursues an issue to achieve results while at the same time acting with respect, care, and the fairness for the well-being of all the people involved in that organization's project.

Box 5.1 Leadership experience with reality

In 1999 I happened to have been an acting executive director of the Council for NGOs in Malawi for a couple months before I left for my studies in Australia. The organization was hierarchically structured. My predecessor, while a learned person, lacked some people skills, in my opinion. It was lunch hour. The "junior staff" often contribute some money to buy maize meal and relish which, instead of each going their way for lunch, they get together during lunch hour to cook and eat together. I noted this practice for a while and, one day, I decided to join them. To my surprise, they "freaked," almost begging me not to join them. This was not because they did not want to share the meal, but that I was a person who belonged to a particular "class" and also an "authority," a "boss" who would not eat what they were eating and interact with them casually. I vividly remember one of them remarking "*Inu bwana mungadye ndi ife?*" (Sir, are you such a person who can eat with us?). While this was not a joke, I was really hungry. However, I also wanted to "come down to earth." I wanted to demonstrate my "human-ness," despite that hierarchically I was at the helm of the organization. I wanted to show that I was human and fully interactive, able to enjoy their company and be as they were.

The perception people have in an organization can shape leadership style. Similarly the perception a leader has in an organization can shape how the rest of the organization operates in development processes. In the case in Box 5.1, not only did I avail myself as an ordinary person but I also enhanced the "social capital" of the so-called "junior staff," who may have considered themselves far distant from the top. Changing the top-down hierarchy to a horizontal structure is what leadership is all about. Values have a powerful influence on the way an organization can operate.

At a time when NDGOs are called upon to be accountable and demonstrate their impact, the importance of visionary leadership cannot be overemphasized. Unfortunately the absence of research into NGO leadership compounds the sector. Hailey and James[22] admit that leadership research has tended to focus on the role and character of leaders in the for-profit sector rather than the non-profit or public sectors. Where research in the sector has taken place, there is much emphasis on the industrialized countries of the North and its non-profit leadership, especially NGO boards.

In the developing world, the burgeoning brand of leadership exhibits a number of traits. One such trait is personalization of leadership which is closely linked to "founder syndrome." While there is no harm in founding an organization, there are, however, fears on how such founders become paternalistic, autocratic and overzealous. That said, still there is scanty evidence on why NDGO leaders in the developing world behave in such a way, and more importantly, the effects of such behavior on their development endeavors.[23] Paternalism is a form of power and very often the founder syndrome, coupled with power, produces an identity the ultimate destiny of which is self-interest and -gratification. Very often it results in what I call "management by distance," meaning that the leader at the helm of an organization leads by ensuring that the distance between their position and those around them is wide enough to maintain the status quo. One can easily find this exhibited in the hierarchical nature in which these organizations are structurally set up.

It is not uncommon to encounter incidents that depict a culture of "bossiness." Decision making in the case above seems to be the prerogative of the leader, an issue that largely highlights organizational leadership that is vertical rather than both vertical and horizontal in nature. I earlier alluded to good NDGO leaders providing an opportunity for leadership to permeate at every level and, more so, allowing every employee to contribute to the vision. This means delegating responsibility, inculcating the spirit of trust and accountability. In Africa, as is the case in other parts of the world, leadership is embedded in cultural practices. James expresses his fear as he notices that there is "a clear cultural approach to leadership that very much fits the stereotypical 'big man' model of African social and political leaders."[24] He also highlights certain features that support the influence of culture on leadership. He identifies traits of "power" where the leadership style is pretty much based on hierarchy and full of dictatorial tendencies. In some cases leadership can be seen as an instrument of engendering order or fear. By not allowing differing views or dissent, a leader can be a fearsome person, someone whose views have to be final. This trait is similar to those that exhibit leaders as all-knowing and all-owning. Such leaders rise above the ethos of an organization and place themselves above everyone else. They are less consultative as they regard themselves to possess all the answers and the wisdom in the world. The persuasiveness of their traits makes some leaders infallible, hence they feel completely prominent in an organization. Such leaders, James observes, are the leaders who take leadership as a personal possession and can stay for life.

While these observations are broad and common in both the political arena and the nongovernmental sector, the pervasiveness of such practices in the sector remains an area of further research. It is especially so when one considers the gender dimension of leadership in the development sector. For example, in most African societies, women are usually subordinate to men. The perception that a woman, for example, has to pay higher respect to a man is a factor that can potentially have an effect on how female-headed NGOs are able to operate in a male-dominated society. Hailey observes that:

> Women leaders face cultural expectations as to their gender roles. In practice this can mean that they face prejudice, harassment, and family pressure and have limited careers expectations ... Women leaders have had to adopt particular coping strategies and proactively manage social expectations so as to be accepted in leadership positions. Women in such leadership roles with deep rooted attributes about the role of women in a society dominated by men.[25]

Box 5.2 Case study: Bougainville

In 2004 I was privileged to undertake my first academic research with a female headed local NGO in post-conflict Bougainville. Emerging out of a secessionist conflict, the organization, inspired by the desire for reconciliation and post-conflict reconstruction, managed to establish itself amidst high level of prejudice. However, the leadership style was firm and culturally entrenched. Bougainville is a matrilineal society. Despite sporadic signs of resistance, the organisation had the support of men. However, one startling discovery was the jealousy amongst other female-headed local NGOs. Partly, the dynamic leadership of this organization based on its network with Australian academics and, also, a female-headed international NGO in Australia, made it reasonably successful given that it had funding.

(Peter Ninnes, Bert Jenkins and Helen Hakena, eds, *NGOs and Post-Conflict Recovery: The Leitana Nehan Women's Development Agency and Peace Building on Bougainville* (Canberra: Pacific Press, 2006))

It is not the intention of this chapter to demonize women but there are lessons that can be drawn from the Bougainville case. Part of being a good leader is to acknowledge that change is a process that affects both genders and, for that matter, in development, it is as crucial. The various definitions of the concepts in Box 5.2 are informed by theories to which I now turn in the next section.

Leadership theories and change in development

So far I have waffled enough in trying to avoid the often popular discourse in the leadership literature. It is becoming increasingly clear that in a time of increasing discourse of "theory of change,"[26] NGO leadership is under constant pressure to resist the old adage of leadership theory. If we just pause for a moment to reflect on the complexity of change, we are bound to ask one fundamental question: "Who ensures that change context, processes, and content relate effectively and that change space engineers to endure readiness for change and adjustment in the change processes?"[27] As would be the case, the most probable response would be "leadership." Essentially it is the role of the leader to effect change. This is what we have so far established.

These claims are reflective of theories that have spanned decades of research in trying to understand the complexity of leadership. Burns,[28] for example, argues that leadership can be appreciated in the context of the change process. Adding to this debate, Linsky and Heifetz[29] argue further and posit that while leadership and change are inseparable bedfellows, leadership should be seen as a facilitative instrument for what they call "adaptive change." So does Yukl, who affirms that change "is the essence of leadership and everything else is secondary."[30]

Perhaps what these scholars are arguing about is what, over the years, has become a fragmented set of theories on leadership often coined from various schools of thought. Andrew and his colleagues sum up their concerns:

> Theorists relate steadfastly to schools of thought that seem exclusive and difficult to integrate, sporting names like "trait theory," the "leadership behaviour school," "power and influence approach," "situational and contingency theory," "constructive leadership and fellowship." These schools tend to posit different arguments in regard to fundamental questions, like: who is the change leader? Why? What does the leader do in the change process? How? How does the context influence leadership in change?[31]

These questions are fundamental in the context of changes propagated by the NGO sector. In the next section I highlight some of the issues with which the current NGO leadership grapples and make propositions based on my personal experience and thinking.

Organizational growth and leadership challenges

The broader discussion in the previous sections has so far theorized leadership management and governance. By the sound of it, it seems pretty clear that the role of leadership is to steer the organization into achieving what it has set out to achieve, but we should not forget that organizations grow. Most development NGOs, especially those from the South, start small and later grow into much larger organizations as their constituencies' needs also expand.[32] Leadership in a nascent organization will differ from an emerging organization. Similarly, leadership in the expanding organization will most likely be different from a mature organization. In all this, NGDOs' developmental stages, the leadership, management and governance processes will have to be adaptive to the changing internal as well as external environment.

Richard Holloway's checklist of NGO organizational development (Table 5.2) has been widely used to highlight the progressive developmental stages NGOs go through. A reflection on a few aspects of governance and management practices may help us understand the challenges and opportunities of the progressive growth of these development organizations, although some of the points he raises are subject to continued research and debate.

Table 5.2 Checklist of NGO organizational development

	Nascent organization	Emerging organization	Expanding organization	Mature organization
GOVERNANCE				
Leadership	There is an individual or a few individuals in the NGO who control most functions	Most decisions are made by the board, sometimes with input from one or two staff members	The NGO's links to its constituency are weak	Senior management's relationship to staff is more consultative and management decisions are delegated
	Management style is directive and staff members provide primarily technical input	Staff has little understanding of how management makes decisions	The NGO views its constituency as passive beneficiaries rather than as potential partners	Staff increasingly understands but is not systematically involved in decision making
	Management does not articulate clearly to staff the NGO's purpose or individual staff members' contribution to the purpose	Leadership is still seen primarily as directive and controlling, rather than providing meaning and enabling self-direction to employees and monitoring their performance	The NGO does not serve as an advocate for its constituency	Leadership understands that its primary role is to provide overall direction and monitor performance, but it is still concerned with control
MANAGEMENT PRACTICES				
Planning	Some planning is carried out but with limited input from staff and constituents	Annual operating plans are developed and reviewed primarily by senior staff without reference to the previous year's planning, analysis of resource availability, or other factors that could affect implementation	Strategic and short-term planning is conducted primarily by senior management	There is an annual review of the NGO's achievements and an analysis of resource availability

(continued on next page)

Table 5.2 (continued)

Nascent organization	Emerging organization	Expanding organization	Mature organization
Decisions are made and activities planned without reference to the agreed-upon strategies to achieve the mission	Annual plans are developed with little or no input from constituents or staff	Staff and constituents may have some input in the planning but they are not involved in decision making	All parts of the organization develop annual operating plans aligned with the NGO's mission and strategies
There is little assessment of the resources required to undertake activities		There is occasional review of work plans	There is regular review of long-term plans
One or a few people may make decisions and plan activities, giving little explanation to those responsible for implementation			

Source: (Adapted from Richard Holloway, "Establishing and Running an Advocacy NGO," 1998, www.akdn.org/publications/civil_society_advocacy_ngo.pdf, 136–37)

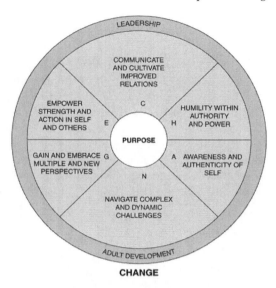

Figure 5.2 Transitional leadership model (Sulpizio Lorri and Robin McCoy, "Transitional Leadership", in *Leadership in Nonprofit Organizations: A Reference Handbook,* ed. Kathryn. A. Agard (Thousand Oaks, Calif.: Sage, 2010), 377–376)

Although Holloway's checklist can be challenged, it provides a basic understanding of organizational growth. There are three issues on which I want to expound.

An organization can espouse all the necessary characteristics of good leadership and/or management but still fail to connect with the community. Kaplan[33] warns that there are times when an NGO gets caught up in the activity trap of the "doing role" yet completely forgets where the organization is going. Even then, knowing where the organization is going is not enough when the focus is the organization.

When an organization is scaling up, what is needed is a type of leadership that also meets the process. In this case, "transitional leadership" seems a perfect fit to deal with such organizational growth.[34] The transitional leadership model is concerned with a successful change that is progressive and smooth. The philosophical foundation of the concept is premised on the belief that:

- leadership is about mobilizing people towards change;
- leadership is about dealing with and managing transitions amid tensions and contradictions; and

- leadership is being focused on purpose because when people know their purpose it is easy to change the course of action.

Being conscious of change is also to realize that any development intervention steered by transitional leadership is going to affect people's norms. This is why transitional leadership is suited to a development organization because not only does it embrace relational leadership, power and awareness, but it is critical for being conscious of others. While transitional leadership has made headways into the organization debate, there has been an equally interesting thrust on the concept of "leaderful," which I discuss in the following section.

Leaderful leadership and development

In the preceding sections I discussed four critical processes of leadership based on a business model.[35] In arguing for the need for "leaderful leadership," Raelin seems to be frustrated with the conventional model of leadership where leadership is serial, individualistic, controlling and dispassionate. I take comfort in knowing that what leaderful leadership espouses is what is also envisioned in post-development thinking.[36] If development is about building relationships, then leaderful leadership is a perfect ingredient to steer development NGOs in a direction of achieving the vision of making poverty history because, as Chambers[37] once said, we have to let go the power and find concurrences, sharing power. Let us also espouse the view of Laurens van der Post, who once said we no longer want to be led from outside. Each of us must be our own leader. We know enough now to follow the light thus within ourselves, and through this light we will create a new community.[38] Not only is van der Post calling for "collective" and "concurrent" action, but he also espouses "collaboration," both of which are fundamental tenets of leaderful leadership. The fourth pillar of leaderful leadership mirrors one of the key foundations of modern development thinking: participation. Raelin sees leaderful leadership as that which embraces "compassion." Raelin argues:

> By demonstrating compassion, one extends unadulterated commitment to preserving the dignity of others ... Each member of the community is valued regardless of his or her background or social standing and all viewpoints are considered regardless of whether they conform to the current thought processes. Compassionate leaders recognize that values are intrinsically interconnected with leaderships and that there is no higher value than democratic participation.[39]

It is by no coincidence, therefore, that Raelin's framework and that of Lorri and McCoy overlap and both seem to support my third issue, that of humanizing leadership through what is known as "servant leadership."

Servant leadership in development NGOs

In an era when NGDOs have come under heavy scrutiny and pressure to demonstrate accountability and transparency, "servant leadership" has gained currency.[40] NGDOs are servants of their constituencies. Their values, which we discussed in the introductory chapter, are the foundations of their work. Servant leadership upholds the morals of humaneness. The idea has developed from various models of leadership. Burns[41] and Greenleaf[42] are associated with the coining of the idea. In particular, Greenleaf's arguments about servant leadership are premised on the philosophical foundation that puts first and foremost the interests and aspirations of other people's need before one's own. Servant leadership is about being a servant to others rather than leading others. Oxymoronically, it seems contradictory that one can be a servant but at the same time lead others. Over the years the concept has undergone some reconceptualization.[43] Being a servant leader is to recognize *who* you are first and *what* you do next.[44] To that end, to serve entails a self-concept where one takes the view that you are in a leadership position with the imperative that you "serve" rather "lead." This requires some form of inner transformation to "selflessness." This is what Burns argues to be another form of servant leadership. Transforming leadership, Burns argues, occurs where "one or more persons engage with others in such a way that leaders and followers raise one another to higher levels of motivation and morality ... [it] becomes *moral* in that it raises the level of human conduct and ethical aspirations of both leader and led, thus it has a transforming effect to both."[45]

Other commentators in the field of leadership theory have also weighed in to take Greenleaf's philosophy to a higher level.[46] The view that leadership transcends social responsibilities resonates much in the literature. While there is an acknowledgment that servant leadership theory lacks empirical evidence,[47] the paradigm shift from a focus on the well-being of an organization to serving followers is what gives the theory its currency.[48] Not only does the people-centered approach make way for a safe and strong relationship with organizations but, as van Dierendonck puts it, "power becomes a possibility to serve others and as such may even be considered a prerequisite for servant-leaders. Serving and leading become almost exchangeable. Being a servant allows a person to lead; being a leader implies a person serves."[49]

The discipline that individuals develop when they espouse servant leadership is a strength that is highly needed in development practice. While development theory is consumed with discourses of empowerment, participation, capacity development and partnership building,[50] servant leadership theory offers new thinking in *humanizing* development by going beyond the "feel good" factor to thinking about human emotions. Development practitioners in NGDOs need to be "humble" and resist the temptation to be "experts,"[51] and learn to unlearn certain practices and admit that they can learn from the communities they serve, and retreat into the background when a task has been successfully accomplished.[52]

So the venture and critique of development practice has failed to engage with the notion of "development ethics." NGO codes of ethics, as discussed earlier, come closer to my argument but fall short of operationalizing the idea. If servant leadership is about "authenticity" then we also need to acknowledge the need for NGDOs to adhere to the moral code of conduct.

Box 5.3 Case study

In 1998 I attended a meeting sponsored by a donor agency on "poverty alleviation in Malawi." My organization had a policy that when someone is travelling on official duties away from their work station they should be paid travel and subsistence allowance. The organizations that called the meeting provided accommodation and lunch. On the day of the meeting I was called to "sign" for another allowance. I refused to sign. The act provoked some resentment among other NGOs on the basis that my thinking represented a significant shift in the popular practice where "signing" is normal; it does not matter how many times one does it. I refused to sign because, first, I had already signed for my organization. Second, I refused to sign because I felt it was selfish to do so. Third, I did not sign because I felt the money could be used for something else, perhaps for the very issue of someone's poverty.

Little did I know in my act (Box 5.3) that I was in actual fact fulfilling one of the servant leadership tenets: "stewardship." As well as a caretaker in my organization, I also demonstrated a model which, despite irritating my fellow NGO leaders, may have had an impact on the way they perceived their role in their respective organizations.

Poverty affects human emotions. Poverty humiliates. When the NDGO operates in an environment where communities are highly affected by poverty, some of the attributes highlighted in servant leadership may be critical. More importantly, in such a situation a combination of attributes from various theoretical orientations may prove effective. Let us take an example of a leader in the case study in Box 5.4.

Box 5.4 Case study

"Chanje" was an NGO established to provide support for the community development in a village in one of the developing countries. The country director was from a different country with a different cultural orientation to the one in which he was working. His employees, being aware of the cultural context and the importance of relationships, were respectful of communities with which they worked. One day the country director joined his team for field work in one of the rural communities. Upon arrival the village head person offered him a brick as a chair. Instead of sitting, he continued to converse while standing. The rest of his team sat on the ground with ease and comfort. Further meetings between the community and the NGO took a different shape as many members of the community never turned up. In one of the meetings organized by the deputy country director, the whispers permeated, indicating the fall-out of recognizing cultural practices. In other words, the actions of the country director showed disrespect to the community and, similarly, a lack of sensitivity to the emotional distress that may have been caused by his lack of appreciation and failure to learn from the context.

While the NGO in the case study may have been comfortable in their service to the community, there was a glaring gap between the leader and his staff which, ultimately, was exposed on the ground. One may ask if there was any learning and/or reflection on what the organization was doing, or similarly if the organization was driven by a particular value-based approach to community engagement.

Conclusion

The chapter set out to examine the importance of good leadership in NGDOs. In summary, the discussion in this chapter has highlighted the fact that there is undeniable evidence that the leadership field is rich with theories, models, techniques and tools, all designed to prepare and nurture individuals both in the public and private sectors to lead. The chapter has brought together some key issues in the debate and highlighted the importance of the theories to the field of development. In particular, NGO leadership has particularly been highlighted as crucial because of its closeness to communities. Today's leaders are facing huge challenges but, at the same time, stand before great opportunities. Communities in both developing and developed countries are no longer the same as they were two decades ago. The very idea of "community" is being redefined as people strive for community change. Amidst all this is the centrality of NDGOs in fostering that change. It is not uncommon, therefore, to note the emphasis in the literature on collective leadership, collaborative leadership, steward leadership and many other forms of leadership which, in all cases, emphasize the type of leadership that crosses many boundaries: that is boundaries between organizations, groups and individuals. Importantly, NGDO leaders need leadership skills that deal with issues that divide communities. This is when the NGDO leaders need to adapt constantly to changing times.

The chapter has also emphasized that NGDO leadership, although loaded with power undertones, should learn to share power not only in their organizations but through ways in which the organizations are seen as vehicles or building blocks for community empowerment. This can only be achieved when organizations (and the people in the organization) learn from practice. Challenging one's own assumptions is what adaptive, collective, servant, and leaderful leaderships are all about. NGDO leadership in the twenty-first century should foster what Raelin calls leaderful practice, where "leadership is being seen more as a plural phenomenon, something that the entire community does together. It does not need to be associated with the actions of a single operator."[53] Put simply, NGDO leadership should facilitate processes in community development efforts where community leaders are encouraged to expand their perspectives from an emphasis on "I" to emphasizing both "I" and "we." This is about learning, and is the focus of Chapter 6.

Notes

1 Bill Newman, *10 Laws of Leadership: Leading to Success in Changing World* (Benin City: Marvellous Christian Publication, 1997).
2 Joseph A. Raelin, *Creating Leaderful Organizations: How to Bring Out Leadership in Everyone* (San Francisco, Calif.: Berrett-Koehler, 2003).
3 Gary A. Yukl, *Leadership in Organizations*, 7th edn (New York: Pearson Prentice Hall, 2010).

4 Allan Kaplan, *Leadership and Management* (Cape Town: CDRA, 1994), www.cdra.org.za/site/articles/Leadership%20and%20Management%20-%20 by%20Allan%20Kaplan.htm.

5 Warren G. Bennis and Burt Nanus, *Leadership: The Strategies for Taking Charge* (New York: Harper & Row, 1985); Mark J. Ahn, John S.A. Adamson and Daniel Dornbusch, "From Leaders to Leadership: Managing Change," *Journal of Leadership and Organisational Studies* 10, no. 4 (2004): 112–23.

6 Kaplan, *Leadership and Management*.

7 Bennis and Nanus, *Leadership: The Strategies for Taking Charge*, 21.

8 John P. Kotter, *Leading Change* (Boston, Mass.: Harvard Business Press, 1996).

9 Afsaneh Nahavandi, *The Art and Science of Leadership*, 3rd edn (Upper Saddle River, N.J.: Prentice Hall, 2003), 4.

10 John Hailey, *NGO Leadership Development: A Review of the Literature*, INTRAC Praxis Paper No. 10. (Oxford: INTRAC, 2006).

11 Newman, *10 Laws of Leadership*, 7.

12 Raelin, *Creating Leaderful Organizations*, 7.

13 Yukl, *Leadership in Organizations* (7th edn).

14 Joseph C. Rost, *Leadership for the Twenty-first Century* (New York: Praeger, 1991).

15 Peter Northouse, *Leadership Theory and Practice* (Thousand Oaks, Calif.: Sage Publications, 2007).

16 ODI, *Governance, Development and Effectiveness: A Quick Guide to Complex Relationships*, 2006, www.odi.org.uk/sites/odi.org.uk/files/odi-assets/publications-opinion-files/218.pdf.

17 Ross Garland, "Developing a Project Governance Framework," cms.3rdgen.info/3rdgen_sites/107/resource/GERLAND_Project_Governance_Paper.pdf.

18 Patrick S. Renz, *Project Governance. Implementing Corporate Governance and Business Ethics in Nonprofit Organizations* (Berlin: Physica Verlag, 2007), 16.

19 Alan Fowler, *Striking a Balance: A Guide to Enhancing the Effectiveness of Non-Governmental Organisations in the International Development* (London: Earthscan, 1997), 234.

20 Centre for Creative Leadership/People in Aid, *Leadership and Talent Development in International Humanitarian and Development Organizations* (Brussels, Belgium: Centre for Creative Leadership and London: People in Aid, 2010), www.ccl.org/leadership/pdf/research/LeadershipTalentDevelopment. pdf, 18.

21 James M. Kouzes and Barry Z. Posner, *The Leadership Challenge*, 3rd edn (San Francisco, Calif.: Jossey-Bass, 2003).

22 John Hailey and Rick James, "'Trees Die from the Top': International Perspectives on NGO Leadership Development," *Voluntas: International Journal of Voluntary and Nonprofit Organizations* 15, no. 4 (2004): 343–53.

23 Rick James, "Leadership Development Inside-Out in Africa," *Non-Profit Management and Leadership* 18, no. 3 (2008): 359–75.

24 James, "Leadership Development Inside-Out in Africa," 365.

25 Hailey, *NGO Leadership Development*, 14–15.

26 INTRAC, "Theory of Change," *Ontrack* 51 (May 2012), www.intrac.org/data/files/resources/741/ONTRAC-51-Theory-of-Change.pdf.

27 Matt Andrew, Jesse McConnell and Alison Wescott, "Development and Leadership-Led Change—A Report for the Global Leadership Initiative and the World Bank Institute," *HKS Faculty Research Working Paper*, RWP10-009, John F. Kennedy School of Government, Harvard University (March 2010), dash.harvard.edu/bitstream/handle/1/4449099/Andrews_Dev elopmentLeadership.pdf?sequence=1.

28 James M. Burns, *Leadership* (New York: Harper and Row Publishers, 1978).

29 Martin Linsky and Ronald A. Heifetz, *Leadership on the Line: Staying Alive through the Dangers of Leading* (Boston, Mass.: Harvard Business School Publications, 2002).

30 Gary A. Yukl, *Leadership in Organizations*, 5th edn (Upper Saddle, N.J.: Prentice Hall, 2002), 273.

31 Andrew *et al.*, "Development and Leadership-Led Change," 10.

32 Richard Holloway, "Establishing and Running an Advocacy NGO," 1998, www.akdn.org/publications/civil_society_advocacy_ngo.pdf.

33 Kaplan, *Leadership and Management*.

34 Sulpizio Lorri and Robin McCoy, "Transitional Leadership," in *Leadership in Nonprofit Organizations: A Reference Handbook*, ed. Kathryn A. Agard (Thousand Oaks, Calif.: Sage, 2010), 377–76.

35 Raelin, *Creating Leaderful Organizations*.

36 Arturo Escobar, *Encountering Development: The Making and Unmaking of the Third World* (Princeton, N.J.: Princeton University Press, 1995); Jonathan J. Makuwira, "Development? Freedom? Whose Development and Freedom?" *Development in Practice* 16, no. 2 (2006): 193–200; Ian Kapoor, *The Postcolonial Politics of Development* (London and New York: Routledge, 2008).

37 Robert Chambers, *Whose Reality Counts: Putting the First Last* (London: Intermediary Technology Publications, 1997).

38 Sir Laurens van der Post said this in an interview with Michael Toms, in 1994.

39 Raelin, *Creating Leaderful Organizations*, 16.

40 Sen Sendjata and James C. Sarros, "Servant Leadership: Its Origin, Development, and Application in Organizations," *Journal of Leadership & Organizational Studies* 2, no. 2 (2002): 57–64.

41 Burns, *Leadership*.

42 Robert K. Greenleaf, *Servant Leadership: A Journey into the Nature of Legitimate Power and Greatness* (New York: Paulist Press, 1977).

43 Max Depree, *Leadership is an Art* (New York: Dell Publishing, 1989); Dirk van Dierendonck, "Servant Leadership: A Review and Synthesis," *Journal of Management* 37, no. 4 (2010): 1228–61; Shann R. Ferch, "Servant-Leadership, Forgiveness, and Social Justice," *International Journal of Servant-Leadership* 1 (2005): 97–113.

44 Sendjata and Sarros, "Servant Leadership."

45 Burns, *Leadership*, 20.

46 van Dierendonck, "Servant Leadership"; Mahalinga S.A. Shiva and Damodar Suer, "Transformational Leadership, Organizational Culture, Organizational Effectiveness, and Program Outcomes in Non-Governmental Organisations," *Voluntas* 23, no. 3 (2012): 684–710; Bruce E. Winston and Barry Ryan, "Servant Leadership as a Humane Orientation: Using the GLOBE Study Construct of Human Orientation to Show Servant Leadership is More Global than Western," *International Journal of Leadership*

Studies 3, no. 2 (2008): 212–22; James W. Sipe and Don M. Frick, *Seven Pillars of Servant Leadership: Practicing the Wisdom of Leading by Serving* (New York: Paulist Press, 2009).

47 Peter Block, "Servant-leadership: Creating an Alternative Future. Keynote address, 2005 International Servant-Leadership Conference, Indianapolis, Indiana, United States of Americas," *International Journal of Servant-Leadership* 2: (2005): 55–79.

48 Gregory A. Stone, Robert F. Russell and Kathleen Patterson, "Transformational Versus Servant Leadership: A Difference in Leader Focus," *Leadership and Organization Development Journal* 25, no. 4 (2004): 349–61.

49 van Dierendonck, "Servant Leadership," 4.

50 Alan Fowler, "Beyond Partnerships: Getting Real About NGO Relationships in the Aid Systems," in *NGO Management*, ed. Michael Edwards and Alan Fowler (London: Earthscan, 2002), 241–55; Jonathan J. Makuwira, "Civil Society Organizations (CSOs) and the Changing Nature of African Politics: The Case of the CSO–Government Relationship in Malawi," *Journal of Asian and African Studies* 46, no. 6 (2011): 615–28.

51 Makuwira, "Civil Society Organizations (CSOs) and the Changing Nature of African Politics."

52 van Dierendonck, "Servant Leadership," 6.

53 Raelin, *Creating Leaderful Organizations*, 113.

6 Shaping NGDOs' moral development crusade through learning

- Learning and NGDOs as learning organizations
- Learning organizations in context
- Organizations as part of a complex social system
- Understanding social change
- Knowledge, social change, and power
- Learning through monitoring and evaluation
- Learning through peer review
- Conclusion

It is not often easy for humans, let alone organizations, to step back and reflect on their actions. In the case of people working in NGDOs, a reflection on their daily experiences and practices is highly critical. Despite the obvious, the call for learning in organizations is by no means easy. Over the past five decades, top-down development approaches have been the hallmark of development practice. These approaches have thrived with limited impact on the daily lives of the poor. The application of one-size-fits-all approaches has come under constant scrutiny as to whether such development strategies add any value in a complex development environment. As a result there has been an increased recognition that development is not a simple undertaking. Rather, development is a process of social change which, in many ways, defies academic theories as well as development models and tools. Thus, in implementing development interventions, the "process" unfolds in a complex terrain of social, political, economic and cultural dynamics. A learning organization will often pay attention to how this process unfolds in order to reflect, learn and plan accordingly. More importantly, "change ... is a given but pro-poor social change efforts require conscious actions."[1]

This chapter seeks to delve deep into and further the debate about "learning organizations" by transcending the simplistic analysis often borrowed from the management field largely associated with the corporate world. The chapter is divided into seven sections, starting with a broader overview of the concept of learning and ways in which NGDOs are learning organizations. The discussion continues with a critical analysis of what learning is all about in development organizations considering that such organizations are part of a complex social system. The rest of the chapter focuses on understanding social change in relation to how development organizations construct knowledge in an environment of competing power dynamics through learning accrued from monitoring, evaluation, and peer review. The chapter aims to unpack the complexity of the debate and expose the subtleties, competing views and perspectives that show that the current debate on "learning organizations" overlooks the fundamental issues of power dynamics and institutional "ordering" of development processes which are often masked by popular discourses of participation and capacity development.

Learning and NGDOs as learning organizations

Why is learning important in a development context? This is a fundamental question that anyone concerned with positive change in a development context ought to be asking. In their paper "Learning Leaders: The Key to Learning Organizations," Hailey and James[2] acknowledge that learning and knowledge management are crucial for the success of NGOs. However, they go further to query why learning is important to NGOs and whether NGOs are natural learners. Importantly, and from a broader context, the question on how successful NGOs actually learn and what distinguishes them from others, is as vital as asking what drives NGOs to desire learning and the role individuals in organizations play in the process. By all means, Hailey and James simply pose these questions essentially to open a conversation which this chapter aims to debate further.

In starting the dialogue on NGDOs as "learning organizations," it is vital that we first navigate through the notion of "learning." A considerable amount of literature abounds on the topic.[3] In this section, I briefly capture a few conceptual issues that underpin learning in a development context. Figure 6.1 sums up various perspectives.

In the face of increasing criticism for lack of impact, accountability and transparency, NGDOs are not only confronted with the challenge of evidence but also demonstrating that they, too, espouse criticism. The definitions in Figure 6.1 provide a set of key issues that underpin learning. Thus, the key features of learning include, but are not limited to:

Process of continual reflection about vision, strategies, actions and relations to capacity for learning. Guijt, 2010.

Dialogue, a process of internal as well as social negotiation. Jonassen, 2003.

How we change and become different from the way we were before. Peddler & Aspinwall, 1998.

LEARNING

Evidence in changed (Improved) action. Knowing is not the same as learning. Taylor, 2006.

A process of continually remaking the mind and to remake and remake it, the mind must first have been made. Jan Visser, 2002, p. 1.

Creative process that cannot be accomplished by a mechanical transfer of external knowledge. Anisur Rahman, cited in Bartby, 2003, p. 89.

Figure 6.1 Conceptual issues underpinning learning (Adapted from James Taylor, "Real Learning Requires Attitude," April 2006, www.cdra. org.za/index.php?option=com_content&view=article&id=57%3A-r eal-learning-requires-attitude&Itemid=2)

- improvement in practice;
- strategic adjustment;
- observable change;
- social process of dialogue and negotiation; and
- rethinking the core driving values of change.

Learning organizations in context

The literature on learning organizations has over the past two decades received much attention.[4] Definitions of learning organizations have varied as the debate has gained ascendancy. Peter Senge,[5] in his book *The Fifth Discipline: The Art and Practice of the Learning Organization*, sees a learning organization as an entity that is adaptive and responsive to past errors and able to transform itself continually.

Senge's work has also given impetus for further analysis. According to Taylor, a learning organization is an "organization which builds and improves its own practice by considering and continually devising and developing the means to draw learning from its own (and other's [sic]) experience."[6] Taylor's definition follows an in-depth critique of NGDOs by Fowler, who earlier observed:

> An almost universal weakness of NGDOs is found within their often limited capacity to learn, adapt and consciously improve the quality of what they do. This is a serious concern because the future usefulness of NGDOs for the world's poor will depend on their ability to overcome their disabilities. Crudely put, if NGDOs do not learn from their experience, they are destined for insignificance and will atrophy as agents of social change. NGDOs urgently need to put in place systems which ensure that they know and learn from what they are achieving—as opposed to what they are doing—and they apply what they learn.[7]

Fowler's remarks have, over the years, triggered a series of studies and analyses about the effectiveness of NGOs as agents of change and poverty reduction.[8] Recently, Brooks World Poverty Institute published a working paper *The Role of NGOs and Civil Society in Development and Poverty Alleviation.*[9] A number of issues are raised and articulated in this paper, but the authors observe that NGOs have become donor-dependent, donor-driven and service provider entities, rather than entities working on structural causes of poverty through participation and bottom-up approaches. The obvious aftermath of this publication has been a public commentary both by development practitioners and theorists. One such commentator is Duncan Green, on whose blog others comment. It is the commentary by Joanna Spratt, titled "Have NGOs lost their way?" that has captured my attention. Spratt makes the following remarks:

> While NGOs have, and do, try to respond to past apprehensions regarding their work, overall it is not clear that this has led to real-world change. Thirteen years ago Michael Edwards wrote an analysis of NGOs similar to the Banks and Hulme paper (but more specifically focused on international NGOs). The fact that

comparable arguments are being repeated today reinforces the concern that NGOs are not translating their internal reflections into change on the ground.

One of the reasons I appreciated the Banks and Hulme paper was because it reflects my observations while working and travelling in the Pacific. The activities of an NGO in a particular village I visited struck me as illustrative. At the community hall there was a blackboard with remnants of a workshop to establish a community crime prevention committee. The smudged chalk articulated who the "youth rep" was, the "women's rep," the "community leader" and the "church leader": a one-size-fits-all approach to participation. Later I asked around about crime in the village. "We have a few drunken youths but not too much else," came the reply. For certain this was not the end of the story on crime, but what people regularly apologized for and complained about during my stay was the lack of water. Communal taps regularly ran dry and only the lucky few with tanks could collect rain water for drinking. Where this community was "'at" was thirsty, not besieged by criminality. Was the crime prevention committee really top-of-the-list for this village, and even if it was, was the establishment of a committee the best way for them to manage it?[10]

Undoubtedly, the remarks and commentaries by Fowler, Banks and Hulme, and Spratt pull together popular observations and challenges not only common to NGOs but other organizations in the public as well as the private sector who often have good intentions but poorly execute their plans without efforts to draw lessons from their practice or actions. A highlight of this is a case study of an international NGO that worked with community-based organizations in Harare, Zimbabwe (Box 6.1).

Box 6.1 INGO and CBO interaction in Harare, Zimbabwe

In 1995, a leading international NGO (INGO) fielded two community organizers in Harare, Zimbabwe, to live and work with residents of two different urban poor areas.[1] In the ensuing months, the organizers unhurriedly tried to encourage "bottom-up" development: understand the local situation, build on the local people's material resources, creativity, knowledge, and views, strengthen local collective action, and facilitate a process in which the communities propose and pursue ideas that are organic to them. The workers did not put any funding into the communities for over a year. However, funds for the projects had been raised from private sources under the banner of community-based, sustainable development.

In 1996, the organizers were told by their regional program manager that they were behind schedule in producing results. The program director stressed that INGO performance criteria required that communities show progress on specific material improvements within one year. Further delays could result in a cut-off of funds, as donors might think the projects were going nowhere.

The organizers, hoping their bosses would come to understand the communities' perspectives and adjust their expectations, resisted pressure from headquarters to spend money. They believed their work would be undermined if the communities realigned their activities to receive outside funds, rather than rallying around a shared vision of a preferred future relying primarily on their own resources. In the end, under pressure to spend the funds and in danger of losing their jobs, the organizers finally relented. The funding tap was turned on, and the INGO reported to donors in 1997 that the projects were reaching their targeted benchmarks.

Note

1 Grant Power, Matthew Maury and Susan Maury, "Operationalising Bottom-Up Learning in International NGOs: Barriers and Alternatives," *Development in Practice* 12, nos. 3 & 4 (2002): 272–84, 272.

The case in point is a classic case of not only issues of whose voice, reality or decision matters but also issues of "power" at play. I shall discuss the theme of power later but, for now, we can appreciate, in this case, "good intentions gone wrong" and, perhaps more importantly, the challenges of development patronage masked as "project management."

Being a learning organization does not just happen. As stated earlier, there have to be efforts—consciously planned. Taylor[11] makes this point clear. He argues that a learning organization is not one that learns, but one that learns consciously. In other words, learning that is planned purposefully. Our daily experiences in our workplaces are part of a learning process. According to Dewey " … not only are experiences the key building blocks of learning, but action is an intrinsic part of the learning cycle; this implies learning by doing as well as a practical understanding of the world."[12] While Dewey's views are contextualized within the broader general education, the principles remain vital in the wider development field where people's experiences vary markedly depending on the context. Moreover, to assume that at some point organizations and the people in them cease to learn is to undermine the dynamics of the world we live in, which is complex, dynamic, messy and complicated. This, in itself, makes us believe that organizations and their people are constantly learning but learning at different levels: at conscious or deliberate and unconscious levels. It is the conscious and deliberate level on which this discussion focuses.

Not surprisingly, NGDOs as learning organizations are under constant pressure to improve practice. As observed by Crawford, Morris, Thomas and Winter,[13] learning is much more than accumulating information. While it is often that knowledge, information and the ability to think critically and analytically are all essential ingredients in a learning process, it is the change in the practice of individuals and organizations that will ultimately show improvements. Improvements happen in a continuous process. This is the "how" of learning. Articulating this point, Taylor notes:

> In the learning organization the process not only becomes more conscious, but also more continuous ... The learning organization recognizes that learning is not a "one-off" activity where you find the ultimate answer and then forget about it and move onto other things. It is understood that learning is a cumulative process which needs to start where you are, and constantly progress at a pace dictated by a combination of your organizational needs of those you serve. Learning builds on itself through improved action, which in turn opens new opportunities for understanding and further learning.[14]

As depicted in Figure 6.2, it seems that the literature on learning organizations is normative in a way, in that it encourages organizations constantly to go beyond "single-loop learning" where the process of learning is essentially focused on detecting and correcting any deviations from the organization norms and behaviors in order to increase organizational efficiency.[15] Taylor's position calls for learning that reflects multiplicity of actions that transcend single-loop learning to "double-loop learning," where the organization and its employees reflect on the appropriateness of the underlying practices, policies and norms. The premise on which Taylor argues the case is based on the belief that by reflecting on these practices, policies and norms, the organization can avoid repeating similar mistakes. However, even then, questioning organizational underlying practices, policies and norms, without change, does not take the organization far enough unless the

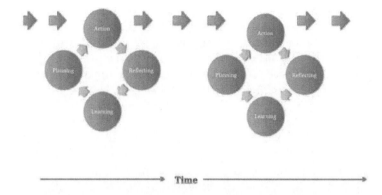

Figure 6.2 Iterative process of organizational learning over time (Adapted from James Taylor, "Real Learning Requires Attitude," April 2006, www. cdra.org.za/index.php?option=com_content&view=article&id=57% 3A-real-learning-requires-attitude&Itemid=2)

learning embraces "triple-loop learning," which is the highest form of organizational self-reflection. It is at this level where the entire organizational culture, rationale and practice are questioned and a conscious decision is made to transform radically the organizational structures and at the same time pay attention to the influence of the external context.[16] While organizations strive to learn, we often ignore the fundamental aspect that organizations exist and operate in a complex social system. The section that follows discusses this notion in order to highlight the linkage between organizations and society.

Organizations as part of a complex social system

The three levels evolutionary model of organizational learning occurs in a complex social process or interaction. I have more than once argued that development is a complex process of social interaction.[17] As such, organizations like NGDOs are critical components of this process, but what constitutes a "learning organization" must be distinguished from "organizational learning," although in some cases the difference between the two may be negligible.

NGDOs as *learning organizations* are enmeshed in a social fabric and do have a culture of their own that deserves analysis in this case. An organizational culture entails the shared beliefs, values, and norms in an organizational context. As Swieringa and Wierdsma[18] observe, culture can determine individual behavior. They further note that culture can also increase the likelihood of learning becoming a natural process that helps to unleash the hidden, basic assumptions and beliefs that are deeply embedded in organizations and are able to develop capacities that can foster double-loop or triple-loop learning.[19] The pragmatism generated out of double-loop and triple-loop learning generates "knowledge for action." This can only happen when such organizations are driven by values that inform praxis. There is one difficulty: that culture cannot be changed or created. Learning organizations can only strive to let culture evolve naturally through new ways of doing and looking at things. This never happens on its own except where an organization develops flexibility and tolerance on how they act upon new information and ideas. Roper and Pettit[20] affirm that such practices can only happen under a set of underlying values which may include the following components:

- valuing different kinds of knowledge and learning styles and creating a "learning environment" so that each organizational member can realize his/her full potential;
- encouraging dialogue and the exploration of different perspectives on experiences to generate creative thinking;
- working collectively and breaking down traditional barriers or blinders within organizations so as to release creative potential; and
- fostering leadership potential throughout the organization and reducing dysfunction such as between management and staff, between strategists and implementers, between support and professional staff, and so on.[21]

The concept of organizational learning, unlike its counterpart learning organization, has its own history. It seems that the literature on this strand of thinking (organizational learning) has been surpassed by one feature that defines learning organization as *action*. Over the past five decades the metamorphosis of the notion of organizational learning has received much attention not only in organizational management but also in the development industry.[22] While the ascendancy of the concept continues to gather pace, especially in the private sector, the key defining feature is centered on "analytic and concentrates on understanding learning processes within organizational settings, without necessarily trying to change those processes."[23] This is not to deny the fact that despite this ontological orientation, organizational learning literature has made a significant contribution to the development field by, for example, highlighting processes of knowledge acquisition and information management; the social fabric of development organizations through analyses of organizational internal politics, conflict, and power dynamics; organizational competitiveness not only from a commercial perspective but also from a sustainability angle; and the psychological and behavioral aspects of individual learning within different cultural contexts in which such organizations operate. The ideological position on which the literature on organizational learning is premised has, undoubtedly, paved the way for a rethinking of new ways to understand learning. In the section that follows I turn to discuss and analyze learning for social change and its implications for development.

Understanding social change

In both the ideal and real world, humans, throughout history, have sought and continue to seek ways and means to bring about social change. However, social change does not occur in isolation because it is a political act, besides being a social process. It comes with possibilities and limitations. Taylor, Deak, Pettit and Vogel[24] have argued that social change is about transformation. If organizations strive to learn because they are driven by a concern about inequality and poverty, then social changes should aim to transform power relationships so that people who are usually on the fringes of society—the powerless poor men and women, the minorities and other excluded groups—are sufficiently mobilized to voice their concerns and be able to influence decisions that affect their lives. However, these are people outside organizations. My focus here is to discuss this in light of people working for development organizations, those who can contribute to social change through radical transformation of internal structures. By any means, these people will need the capacity and skills that enable them to trigger such social change that increases their choices or space to be able to question and understand the "underlying shift in social and cultural norms, values, and worldviews (and the ways in which these are reproduced) as necessary structural and psychological transitions, running parallel to more visible and episodic changes in agency and power relations."[25]

Initiating social change requires knowledge, skills and dynamism because the broad issues of social justice, inequality and poverty involve a range of issues. For example, inequality or poverty is multi-dimensional and, as Jackson[26] argues, it cannot be the preserve of a single dimension. In part, it is because social consciousness still trails behind development, which continues to place economics at the expense of social relations in our society today. Therefore the kind of difference social action and/or change can make, O'Gorman[27] argues, is dependent on:

- understanding what impels society, and in whose interest change takes place;
- perceiving the causes underlying people's poverty;
- valuing the intrinsic dignity of human life; and
- stretching the boundaries of limits of change.

All of the above requires knowledge and understanding of the complexity of social interaction. When organizations reflect on their practice, they generate knowledge. In what ways, then, can knowledge, social change and power be harnessed for the benefit of enhancing NGDOs' moral crusade against poverty? The next section discusses this in more depth.

Knowledge, social change, and power

A mere mention of learning organizations evokes debate about knowledge creation or production. The process of reflection is, by and large, a process of knowledge creation. What is fundamental, then, is to know who creates this knowledge (who is expected to learn), what purpose the creation of knowledge serves, and at what level of an organization is learning aimed.[28] Given that almost every organization is structurally hierarchical, the level at which learning is targeted will also dictate whose knowledge matters in the organization. The challenge goes further than this, especially in development organizations where people rarely ever question or discuss issues of power. Yet, in the broader scheme of things, power relations are seen as obstacles to poverty reduction and inequality.[29]

The literature on organizational learning sheds light on two fronts in relation to power dynamics in organizations. First, there is the *technical* perspective which assumes that the management, processing and interpretation of information matter in organizational learning, and that an organization can pick and choose which information it finds useful. It is the *social* perspective which, for most of its theoretical underpinnings, presents a compelling argument on which I want to reflect. According to this perspective, learning emerges from social relationships and/or interactions and is highly political as well as dependent on organizational culture. Inevitably, it implies that organizations such as NGDOs oftentimes undergo a period of conflict and power struggle, which has to be understood as part of a learning process. If learning is the acquisition of knowledge, and if knowledge is the sense people make of information, and if ultimately knowledge is power, it is then possible that different organizations will value learning or knowledge differently.

They will even go as far as to not reveal knowledge or facilitate learning which, in the end, paves the way or empowers people to challenge the status quo or those in a position of power.[30]

In his paper "Learning from Power in Development Cooperation: Lessons from Senegal," Blane Harvey[31] presents a compelling illustration of the challenges of inter-institutional power relations where managerial discourses and informal learning coalesce within a network of development actors and practitioners. His analysis takes a Foucauldian stance and resonates with the views of Foucault who, in his presentation in "Prison Talk," emphasizes that power sweeps into the very grain of individuals, reaches right into their bodies, permeates their gestures, their postures, what they say, how they learn to live and work with other people. It is the relevance of this contextual understanding of the role of power in development organizations that helps to unsettle the dynamics of knowledge creation and appropriation. Harvey's paper also engages, at length, the work of Pettit,[32] who acknowledges that "understanding and addressing power calls for innovative learning processes, which stimulate not only the conceptual and rational re-evaluation of one's assumed perspective, but also the more experiential, embodied, creative, practical and other non-dialogical means of reflection, or making sense of one's experience of power, and of realizing one's capacity to shift power."[33] The case study Harvey presents in his paper is not uncommon to the Southern NGOs whose funding base is the Northern donor agencies whose influence on local contexts determines whose knowledge matters. This is highlighted in the case study of ENDA Senegal (Box 6.2).

Box 6.2 Case study: ENDA Senegal

ENDA was established in 1972 as a project of the Institute for Economic Development and Planning (IDEP), funded by the recently created United Nations Environment Programme (UNEP), and the Swedish International Development Agency (SIDA). ENDA's establishment is the result of a long journey to enlightened accomplishments having seen the failed development of the South after a decade of independence and a system too fragmented and unfamiliar with the realities of a "third world" that impoverished a little more every day. Since then ENDA has grown into one of the largest Southern-based NGOs worldwide. ENDA has been a pioneer in its methods and in its themes of intervention, and served as a model for many organizations present today in what is now known as the developing world.

Born in the South, to serve the people of the South, ENDA has always conducted its struggle against the socio-economic marginalization of the less fortunate and for sustainable development, mainly at two levels. First, in regard to the basis for improving the living conditions of vulnerable groups such as people living in deprived urban and rural populations in developing countries. Second, taking an active part in the battle of ideas, even in knowledge management, which involves an unwavering commitment to the struggle against the hegemony of neoliberal single thought, action research for development, strengthening capacities of stakeholders, lobbying and advocacy at international conferences (on fair trade, the World Trade Organization negotiations, debt cancellation, respect for human rights, child exploitation, violence against women, etc.

Accompanying its growth and spreading engagement in the South (particularly in West Africa) has been a growing recognition of the institution as a "center of excellence" for partnerships with international and intergovernmental organizations including UN agencies, the World Bank, and others. This has presented an ever-expanding range of new opportunities for partnership and engagement, but has, at the same time, introduced challenges to the retention of its clear and locally oriented vision for social change amid the growing "intellectual hegemony"[1] of institutionalized development practice.

Balancing resistance and viability

The mediation of tensions between external pressures from institutional partners and the institute's own articulation of meaningful social engagement teams presented challenges, but also opened opportunities for collective reflection and informal learning. In the case of one ENDA team, this took the form of weekly meetings for reviewing current and upcoming work—meetings which occasionally shifted to debates over the direction in which particular initiatives were leading the team. Other examples include collaborative research with Northern institutions which attempted to shift the focus of contracted research toward issues that contravened ENDA's core principles (such as the promotion of nuclear energy as "clean energy"); partnerships seeking to engage them as a community intermediary for the introduction of potentially objectionable initiatives (such as large-scale biofuels projects); and invitations to work with Northern research institutions that have previously engaged in highly extractive forms of collaboration with ENDA.

This points to ways that opportunities for relatively open discussion and debate over the broader question of program direction sometimes afforded by the team's weekly meetings served an important and often unacknowledged purpose. On those occasions when the team was allowed (or allowed itself) to forego the expediency of running through the agenda of "to-do" items for the week and delve into the messier and less immediate questions of direction and principles, members were able to challenge each other's views, present arguments for their positions based upon their interpretation of ENDA's purpose, on their own experiences, or on their understanding of local needs and concerns. In doing so they reflected upon and began to assert its agency in the face of external pressure, and helped shape the contemporary identity of the team and the institution more broadly. Conversely, it seemed that those moments where the opportunity to delve into greater detail about such thorny questions was passed over for the sake of concision or expediency (perhaps, for example, in avoiding an extended discussion around the principles that might govern engagement with outside institutions) represented most opportunities for collective learning and strengthening of solidarity within the team.

Some of the key challenges that have emerged include engaging and retaining staff members committed to developing transformative and experimental approaches to effecting change amid this broader climate of homogenization of development practice; maintaining a spirit of collaboration within and between ENDA's teams rather than the free market-inspired competitiveness that current funding protocols have encouraged; and balancing resistance to dominant development frameworks in favor of locally articulated alternatives while remaining accessible to funders upon whose funding their work depends. It is through their engagement with these networks of differently situated actors and their accompanying protocols that the team both shaped and defended its identity.

The institutional challenges noted here represent a site of struggle within the institution and its teams where the constancy of external pressure and micro-technologies of institutional power threaten to uproot and de-legitimize the transformative potential of critical and creative social engagement. Driving and giving direction to this resistance within the team is a (sometimes sporadic) critical reflection over the principles and theories that the team wishes to uphold, the threats to these principles and appropriate responses. If, as their principles suggest, one of the institute's aims is to help people bring about changes in power relations through critical reflection and learning about themselves and their environment better to understand the obstacles they face, then it would seem that more dedicated attention on this resistance within the team could serve as an important starting point.

Note

1 Robert Chambers and Jethro Pettit, "Shifting Power to Make a Difference," in *Inclusive Aid: Changing Power and Relationships in International Development*, ed. Leslie Groves and Rachel Hinton (London: Earthscan, 2004).

Learning in an organizational setting, especially where the organization is immensely influenced by external forces, requires a high level of engaging political lens. While it is desirable to learn as individuals, it is collective efforts that together amount to a force, where collective efforts drive an agenda to move an organization in a positive direction. It also takes special skills to analyze issues more technically. This is what Roche and Kelly[34] call "working politically" by recognizing the importance of informal relationships and institutions.

The structures through which reflective learning takes place have to be both formal and informal but, more importantly, they have to provide a platform on which trust among members of staff is encouraged, and differing views and ideas are expressed freely—even dissenting views. The case of ENDA Senegal reflects an organization that is anchored on the values of social justice by standing for the marginalized people in society—those whose voices may hardly be heard by dominant structures. It is a balancing act to maintain organizational integrity amidst strong external influence camouflaged as partnerships. However, as can be seen in Box 6.2, a conscious decision to open and encourage weekly reflective conversations on both routine and non-routine matters has helped the organization to move beyond "doing" development to learning as a group and valuing each other as a resource. At the same time, such discussion is also unfolding amid an environment buttressed by the participation of other partners such as donors. This gives the organization a sense of ownership in a process of learning though reflection.

Learning through monitoring and evaluation

This section does not intend to delve into the traditional debates about monitoring and evaluation. Rather, I aim to examine critically the role of transformative learning in evaluation. In the previous section reference was made to the effect that the purpose of learning from experience was to avoid repeating mistakes and, if any, improve on the current practice. Despite the popular slogan that "history repeats itself," it is my view that this is not always the case. However, if we look at this from a different angle, those who do not know history are condemned to repeat it.

In everyday lives, our experiences differ. What makes them differ is that the situations in which we accumulate our experiences also differ. Therefore, the applications of learning from experience may have to be carefully considered as they can be deceptive. What has worked in one context may not work in another. However, the costs of not learning from experience can be huge. While we may know our history and use it for learning, the historical contexts may also be highly misleading. As such, historical experiences happen in different contexts such that the application of lessons learnt should also be carefully considered. However, putting the two diametrically opposing views together, we can only say that there is something in between that offers learning through a reflective process.

The purpose of program evaluation is to provide feedback and create positive and sustainable change.[35] Unfortunately while there is a desire to accommodate lessons for improvement, there are times when evaluation is used as a judgment tool or a policing instrument. Oftentimes, it is out of evaluations that development programs may be curtailed to pave the way for new ones. This trend can be a terrifying experience to members of staff in an organization and one that is most likely to create fear of evaluations rather than taking them as a learning opportunity. In this case, organizational change is required to allow monitoring and evaluation processes to be of value, or put simply, a tool for learning, but how can this be done?

The starting point in the use of monitoring and evaluation as learning tools is to acknowledge and appreciate the transformative process accrued from undertaking an evaluation. By "transformative change" I mean change in the organizational structure, culture and purpose. This change, by all means, must involve *all* major stakeholders involved in the change process. This, in a development process, is the involvement of the beneficiaries—the target of the development programs. Importantly, this must happen throughout the project cycle—from project identification, planning, design, implementation, monitoring and evaluation.

Another important aspect of the use of evaluation as learning emanates from the definition of evaluation itself. Patton defines evaluation as a "systematic collection of information about activities, characteristics, and outcomes of programs to make judgments about programs, improve program effectiveness and/or inform decisions about future programming."[36] The definition conveys three fundamental principles critical to learning. First, the process of an evaluation has to be systematic; second, it has to be purposeful; and third, it has to provide useful information for the intended uses.

Bound within the three principles, evaluations can be catalysts to organizational learning and change. The challenge that exists in many development organizations is that rarely are evaluation results used. Where they are, they can enhance organizations to make informed decisions, improve practice, develop new programs, improve the capacity of individuals and enhance organizational learning.[37]

Very often there is a tendency to think that lessons can only be learnt from a development program when it has come to an end. The "process" of implementing a development program is as critical as is the output or outcome. Likewise, the process of conducting an evaluation is as critical to learning as are the cumulative lessons. Patton elucidates the point by noting that:

> Individual changes in thinking and behavior, and program or organizational changes in the procedures and culture, that occur among those involved in evaluation as a result of the learning that occurs during the process. Evidence of process use is represented by the following kind of statement after an evaluation: The impact on our program came not just for the findings but also from going through the thinking process that evaluation required.[38]

Patton's sentiments may sound easy but, as earlier stated, the term evaluation carries with it connotations of being scrutinized, inspected or judged. This is purely human but, on a positive side of this negativity, an evaluation can be positively welcome by members of a development program when the purpose of the evaluation is made clear right at the outset, and also when it is highly inclusive.

In order to optimize learning, evaluations have to employ a transformative model evaluation where participants are encouraged to develop a positive attitude towards change. In this case Boverie and Kroth's[39] transformative model evaluation is used. The model operates on three interrelated levels, as shown in Table 6.1.

In the world of practice, developing awareness may not necessarily be a problem, at least from an individual perspective. The challenge that

Table 6.1 Transformative model evaluation

Steps	Purpose
Awareness	Develop understanding and awareness of what is important
Acceptance	Develop strategies, skills and the environment required to obtain goals
Adaptation	Build sustainability through encouraging risk taking, learning, and building beliefs about the capability of success

Source: (Adapted from Patricia Boverie and Barbara Portzline, *The Role of Transformational Learning in Evaluation: Helping to Increase Positive Attitudes and Sustainability of Programs*, paper presented at the Eighth International Transformative Learning Conference, Hamilton Hotel, Bermuda (November, 2009), 40–41, www.docstoc.com/docs/46769655/TLC-(2009)-Conference-Procee dings-Bermuda–Columbia-University-Teachers-College-Department-of-Organi zation-and-Leadership-Adult-Learning-and–Leadership-Program)

exists in many organizations is to know that you are learning as an individual or as an organization. Furthermore, if there is learning, it is "how" one is learning that matters, otherwise it is practically impossible to develop any strategies in a project the ownership of which is not clearly known. Smit[40] asserts that even when everyone in an organization learns, it does not mean that the organization is improving in its operational behavior. In other words, the "transformation" is not automatic.

Box 6.3 Case study of Participatory Methodologies Forum of Kenya (PAMFORK)

PAMFORK is a network and consulting organization established in 2007 as a five-year research project. It was formed as an all-inclusive network of practitioners driven by their passion for participatory development methodologies. PAMFORK had four main areas of focus:

- awareness raising on the importance of knowledge development and its contested nature;
- promotion and investment of the use of "Southern" knowledge production and emerging practices;
- creating innovative ways to engage the development sector on emerging development practices through research; and
- finding, testing, creating and documenting ideas for processes and tools that will illustrate issues affecting how knowledge is used in development work.

Driven by the vision of social change, PAMFORK engaged in action learning processes with civil society and public-sector organizations by providing advice, facilitation skills, action research, capacity development and training, and information dissemination. Throughout the project, PAMFORK accumulated a lot of issues and lessons through studying a number of cases of good practice, innovations and lessons in participatory development.

By and large, while many INGOs in Kenya strive to achieve their goals by promoting participatory methodologies, the results vary according to organization. For example, PAMFORK's case studies reveal that different organizations have different approaches in knowledge management, storage, retrieval, learning and management processes. Overall, the major lessons documented in the case studies seem to indicate a tendency for INGOs not to document learning/lessons due to various work cultures and institutional challenges. Furthermore, there is a focus on "implementation" at the expense of reflection, learning and action. Also, those organizations that strive to document lessons seem not to have systematic mechanisms to encourage the use of information both internally and externally.

Very few organizations have managed to put systems in place that allow staff members to get together and talk, share and reflect on their experiences. However, overall there is a lot of information that is generated through participatory methodologies that is not well documented and utilized for better development outcomes.
(Stephen Kirimi and Eliud Wakwabubi, *Learning from Promoting and Using Participation: The Case of International Development Organizations in Kenya*, PAMFORK-IKM Working Paper No. 6 (October 2009), wiki.ikmemergent.net/files/IKM-Working Paper-6-PAMFORK-final.pdf)

As the case study of PAMFORK highlighted (Box 6.3), it is becoming increasingly clear that while there is recognition of the potential for enhancing development impact through knowledge management and learning, the institutionalization of these processes as working cultures is far from being real in NGDOs. This, again, is not because there is not enough awareness of the merits of learning but, overall, the challenges are institutional due to the fact that such practices are not fully and consciously embedded in the overall organizational plans and programs. In other words, the absence of inclusion of deliberate efforts to document and manage information is symptomatic of poor development planning.

However, there is considerable recognition in development organizations that one way of increasing learning is through peer review—an issue I now turn to in the next section.

Learning through peer review

The rationale for learning in development organizations is to maximize impact. So far, it is becoming increasingly clear that there are merits in reflecting and acting on new and emerging lessons. One such process can be solicited from peer review. While it is predominantly a research strategy, peer review and its application in international development is poorly understood.[41] In peer review, the purpose is to engage in a process whereby two or more different entities undertake a systematic examination and assessment of each other's performance with the ultimate aim of helping the reviewed entities improve their policy making, adopt best practices, and comply with established standards and principles.[42]

While the definition offers a broader understanding of what peer review achieves, it can also be misleading in that the adoption of best practices can be a subjective thing as contexts vary and the environment within which development takes place is dynamic due to both external and internal factors. In addition, the issue of compliance needs to be handled with caution as the new lessons could be more robust than the standards already set. It is not a *must* that lessons documented should affirm the standards and principles. The idea of peer review can also be used to update such principles and standards.

The peer review mechanism reflects participatory action research (PAR), which follows a cyclical process of "planning," "acting," "observing" and "reflecting."

The fundamental principles of participatory action research are to enhance social justice and change, participation, empowerment, collaboration, relationship building, and bottom-up development processes. In peer review, therefore, some of these principles apply. For example, peer review is driven by principles of trust, mutuality, honesty, collaboration, learning, value sharing, credibility, commitment, neutrality, confidentiality and voluntary spirit.

Between October and December 2011, Oxfam Australia undertook a peer review process of their WASH Program in Bangladesh, Cambodia, Papua New Guinea, Timor Leste, Mozambique, and Zambia. Not only was the purpose to enhance linkages between countries, but also to facilitate and share learning and document lessons. During the *planning* stage, the emphasis was to establish aims and objectives, setting expectations and negotiating a memorandum of understanding (MoU).

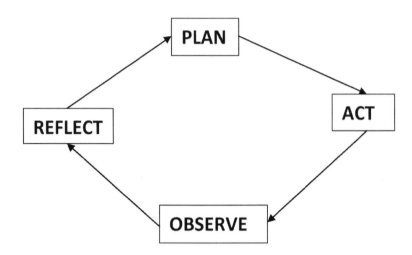

Figure 6.3 PAR principles (N. Godden and Chrisanta Muli, "Peer Review: An Emergent Research within International Development," paper presented at the 3rd ACFID—Universities Linkages Conference, November 2012, Australian National University, Canberra)

In the *acting* stage the review team from one country visited the host country for five days, during which time data were collected using various tools such as individual and group interviews, observations and journals. During the *observation* stage the focus was on noting changes in the practices and the impact such changes had had on development initiatives. Finally, the *reflection* stage included reflecting on the emerging issues and lessons and integrating such changes into programmatic planning. Review could take different forms.

- entity 1 peer reviews entity 2 (Zambia peer reviews Mozambique) (singular peer review);
- entity 1 peer reviews entity 2 and vice versa (Zambia peer reviews Mozambique and vice-versa) (bilateral peer review); or
- entity 1 & 3 peer review, entity 2 & 5 peer review, and entity 4 & 6 peer review (multilateral peer reviews).

While the peer review mechanisms are becoming popular, they are challenging in a number of ways. First, they require more time. Second, they can pose logistical challenges. Third, they are difficult when dealing with language and cultural differences. Despite these challenges, they offer knowledge building, relationship building and confidence building, and enhanced accountability and transparency.[43]

Conclusion

The case studies and literature in this chapter have highlighted that learning in development organizations is not as easy as we might think. Without demonizing "action," we can acknowledge that learning is a complex process because it takes an individual decision to actually dedicate to a change process. Facilitating a process where people in an organization, situated in a very complex cultural milieu, learn to unlearn certain things, can pose a practical challenge. In the first place, people in an organization may not find it easy or necessary if the purpose of the learning is not made clear. In this chapter there is an emphasis on making learning an institutional culture—in other words, learning with a purpose. Development organizations, in other words, have to embed in their mission and vision statements that planning, acting, reflecting and learning are part and parcel of the organizational culture.

If we consider learning in a project setting, then a strategic part of any improved learning is to know how development projects can sometimes garner people's passions and commitment to act. It is also equally vital to consider people's authorities and how such authorities can influence or impact upon learning not only at an individual or organizational level but also to those that the project purports to serve. Sense[44] states that project stakeholders are political players. Paying attention to this trait matters especially in a development project setting. It is very important in enhancing learning. Very often such behaviors can potentially inhibit the exchange of ideas and knowledge flow because of their "influential" status in the community.

The chapter has further highlighted that the most crucial aspect of learning in NGDOs rests in undemanding relations and how these relationships are essential building blocks to learning. Development organizations have a social contract to their constituencies and are, indeed, (at least theoretically) accountable to them. This is a very important site of play in a development process. People in a community are not entirely devoid of knowledge. In fact, they are in most cases more aware of their environment than those who claim to be experts. As noted in this chapter, there are layers of power in those communities. Therefore, while NGDOs may take necessary steps to engage in learning at an organizational level, the milieu from which they draw their lessons is the community itself. As such, NGDO learning should have a balanced view in accommodating community and/or any indigenous knowledge.

This is a conscious decision that has to be made and accommodated as part of a broader scheme that values learning as a conscious decision for change. I conclude this book, in Chapter 7, by pulling together some of the critical issues raised and proposing the way forward for the nongovernmental development sector in our time.

Notes

1 Irene Guijt, *Assessing and Learning for Social Change: A Discussion Paper* (Brighton: IDS, 2007), www.ids.ac.uk/files/dmfile/ASClowresfinalversion.pdf, 4.
2 John Hailey and Rick James, "Learning Leaders: The Key to Learning Organisations," *Development in Practice* 12, nos. 3 and 4 (2002): 398–408.
3 Michael Edwards, "Organisational Learning in Non-Governmental Organisations: What Have We Learnt?" *Public Administration and Development* 17, no. 2 (1997): 235–50; James Taylor, "Real Learning Requires Attitude," April 2006, www.cdra.org.za/index.php?option=com_content&view=article &id=57%3A-real-learning-requires-attitude& Itemid=2; Katy Oswald and Peter Taylor, "A Learning Approach to Monitoring and Evaluation," *IDS Bulletin* 41, no. 6 (2010): 114–20.
4 James Taylor, "NGOs as Learning Organisations," 1998, www.cdra.org.za/ index.php?option=com_content&view=article&id=39%3A-ngos-as-learning -organisations&Itemid=2; Bruce Britton, "The Learning NGO," INTRAC Occasional Paper Series Number 17 (Oxford: INTRAC, 1998); Guijt, *Assessing and Learning for Social Change*; Arja Aarnoudse and Sandra Hill, "Organizational Learning-Purpose, Thinking and Practice: A Literature Survey," 2011, www.pso.nl/files/Publication%20Organisational%20Lear ning,%20a%20literature%20survey_2.pdf.
5 Peter Senge, *The Fifth Discipline: The Art and Practice of the Learning Organization* (New York: Doubleday, 1990).
6 Taylor, "NGOs as Learning Organisations," 64.
7 Alan Fowler, *Striking a Balance: A Guide to Enhancing the Effectiveness of Non-Governmental Organisations in International Development* (London: Earthscan, 1997), 64.
8 David Lewis and Nankeen Kanji, *Non-Governmental Organisations and Development* (London: Routledge, 2009); Jonathan J. Makuwira, "Civil Society Organizations (CSOs) and the Changing Nature of African Politics: The Case of the CSO–Government Relationship in Malawi," *Journal of Asian and African Studies* 46, no. 6 (2011): 615–28.
9 Nicole Banks and David Hulme, *The Role of NGOs and Civil Society in Development and Poverty Alleviation*, Working Paper 171 (Manchester: Brooks World Poverty Institute, 2012).
10 See devpolicy.org/have-ngos-lost-their-way/.
11 Taylor, "NGOs as Learning Organisations."
12 John Dewey, *Experience and Education* (New York: Touchstone, 1997 [1983]).
13 Lynn Crawford, Peter Morris, Janice Thomas and Mark Winter, "Practitioner Development: From Trained Technicians to Reflective Practitioners," *International Journal of Project Management* 24 (2006): 722–33.

14 Taylor, "NGOs as Learning Organisations," 1.
15 Laura Roper and Jethro Pettit, "Development and the Learning Organisation: An Introduction," *Development in Practice* 12, no. 3–4 (2002): 258–71.
16 Britton, "The Learning NGO"; Chris Argyris, *Overcoming Organisational Defenses: Facilitating Organisational Learning* (Boston, Mass.: Allyn & Bacon, 1990); Senge, *The Fifth Discipline.*
17 Makuwira, "Civil Society Organizations (CSOs) and the Changing Nature of African Politics."
18 Joop Swieringa and Andre Wierdsma, *Becoming a Learning Organisation* (Wokingham: Addison-Wesley Publishing, 1992).
19 Chris Argyris and Donald A. Schon, *Organisational Learning: A Theory of Action Perspective* (Reading: Addison-Wesley, 1978).
20 Roper and Pettit, "Development and the Learning Organisation."
21 Roper and Pettit, "Development and the Learning Organisation," 2–3.
22 George P. Huber, "Organisational Learning: The Contributing Processes and the Literature," *Organisational Science* 2, no. 1 (1991): 88–115; Mark Easterby-Smith, "Disciplines of Organisational Learning: Contributions and Critiques," *Human Relations* 50, no. 9 (1997): 1085–2013; Roper and Pettit, "Development and the Learning Organisation"; Kath Pasteur, Jethro Pettit and Boudy van Schagen, "Knowledge Management and Organizational Learning for Development," from *Knowledge Management for Development Workshop* (Brighton: Institute of Development Studies, 2006).
23 Easterby-Smith, "Disciplines of Organisational Learning," 1086.
24 Peter Taylor, Andrew Deak, Jethro Pettit and Isabel Vogel, *Learning for Social Change: Exploring Concepts, Methods and Practice* (Sussex: IDS, 2006), www.ids.ac.uk/files/dmfile/FLASC.pdf.
25 Taylor *et al.*, *Learning for Social Change*, 8.
26 Cecile Jackson, "Disciplining Gender?" *World Development* 30, no. 3 (2002): 497–509.
27 Frances O'Gorman, *Charity and Change* (Melbourne: World Vision Australia, 1992).
28 Guijt, *Assessing and Learning for Social Change.*
29 Jethro Pettit, "Multiple Faces of Power and Learning," *IDS Bulletin* 41, no. 3 (2010): 25–35.
30 Oswald and Taylor, "A Learning Approach to Monitoring and Evaluation."
31 Blane Harvey, "Learning from Power in Development Cooperation: Lessons from Senegal," *Journal of Alternative Perspectives in the Social Sciences* 2, (special issue) no. 1 (2010): 340–71.
32 Jethro Pettit, "Power and Pedagogy: Learning for Reflective Development Practice," *IDS Bulletin* 37 no. 5 (2006): 69–78.
33 Pettit, "Power and Pedagogy"; Harvey, "Learning from Power in Development Cooperation," 344.
34 Chris Roche and Linda Kelly, "Monitoring and Evaluation when Politics Matter," DLP Working Paper 12 (November 2012), www.dlprog.org/ftp/info/Public%20Folder/Monitoring%20and%20Evaluation%20when%20Politics%20Matters.pdf.html.
35 Patricia Boverie and Barbara Portzline, "The Role of Transformational Learning in Evaluation: Helping to Increase Positive Attitudes and Sustainability of Programs," Paper presented at the eighth International Transformative Learning Conference, Hamilton Hotel, Bermuda, November

2009, www.docstoc.com/docs/46769655/TLC-(2009)-Conference-Proceedings-B ermuda-Columbia-University-Teachers-College-Department-of-Organization-a nd-Leadership-Adult-Learning-and-Leadership-Program; Sue C. Funnell and Patricia J. Rogers, *Program Theory: Effective Use of Theories of Change and Logic Models* (San Francisco, Calif.: Jossey-Bass, 2011).

36 Michael Q. Patton, *Utilization-Focused Evaluation: The New Century Text* (Thousand Oaks, Calif.: Sage Publications, 1997), 23.

37 Patton, *Utilization-Focused Evaluation*; Michael Q. Patton, *Essentials of Utilization-Focused Evaluation* (London: Sage, 2012); Hallie S. Preskill and Rosalie T. Torres, *Evaluative Inquiry for Learning in Organizations* (Thousand Oaks, Calif.: Sage Publications, 1999).

38 Patton, *Utilization-Focused Evaluation*, 90.

39 Patricia Boverie and Michael Kroth, *Transforming Work: The Five Keys to Achieving Trust* (Cambridge, Mass.: Perseus Publishing, 2001).

40 Maaike Smit, *We're Too Much in "To Do Mode": Action Research into Supporting International NGOs to Learn*, INTRAC Praxis Paper No. 16 (Oxford: INTRAC, 2007), www.intrac.org/resources.php?action=resource& id=413.

41 N. Godden and Chrisanta Muli, "Peer Review: An Emergent Research within International Development," Paper presented at the 3rd ACFID–Universities Linkages Conference, November 2012, Australian National University, Canberra.

42 OECD, *Peer Review: A Tool for Cooperation and Change*, OECD Policy Brief, 2003, www.oecd.org/eco/22350184.pdf.

43 Godden and Muli, "Peer Review."

44 Andrew J. Sense, "The Conditioning of Project Participants' Authority to Learn within Projects," *International Journal of Project Management* 26, no. 2 (2008): 105–11.

7 Conclusion

The future of the NGDO sector in poverty reduction

- **Lessons: understanding poverty and why a crusade against poverty**
- **Lesson 1: revisiting the aid debate and how NGDOs can manage it**
- **Lesson 2: the management of partnerships and capacity development issues**
- **Lesson 3: leadership and learning**
- **More needs to be done**
- **Final thought**

This book has examined key issues with which NGDOs are grappling in the modern era. As discussed in Chapter 1, NGDOs' ascendancy to their current status has a long history. Over the years, NGDOs have become significant players in the development field through their proximity to their constituencies. While most of the early generations of NGOs were formed to respond to humanitarian needs, this role became more diffuse and, as a result, the expansion to respond to other needs became more inevitable. After World War I and World War II many of these NGOs scaled up their roles from relief and rehabilitation to more social development. This role has meant that most of the NGOs have focused on service provision by filling in the gaps left by governments of the day. As a result, because of limited resources, especially funding, the majority of these NGOs have depended on donors for their development programs. The funding mechanisms espoused by these donors are complex because of the conditions attached.

Chapter 2 highlighted that the concept of partnership has now become a lynchpin of the development discourse. It is becoming increasingly clear that while the current trend is centered around building up alliances in order to maximize impact, the practicalities of this are not as easy as we may think. As noted by Nikolas Barry-Shaw and Dru Oja Jay,[1] for Southern NGOs, the nature of partnerships is not as expected. The power imbalances often inherent in these partnerships have been the highlight of the chapters. Different types of partnerships have their own merits and demerits and can only be judged by the context within which they are taking place. However, as the chapter hinted, there are underlying principles that dictate effective partnerships such as mutuality, reciprocity, trust, two-way communication, transparency, mutual accountability and learning from each other, just to name a few.

Aside from the partnership debate, Chapter 3 centered on the notion of capacity development. The discussion made a critique of competing views of the meanings and how the idea is implemented in practice. As a form of empowerment, capacity development allows people to take control of their destinies and is a highly political process of awareness raising. The chapter highlighted that there is no single way to capacity development, given that NGDOs or institutions are different and operate in different contexts. There is no end to capacity building. It takes time to build and develop sustainable capacities. Fundamentally, capacity building is premised on changing power dynamics. The emphasis has also been that good capacity development builds on existing capacities rather than destroying people's potential. In so doing, I have argued, we focus both on the visible and invisible aspects of the communities we serve.

In Chapter 4 I explored the concept of accountability and how NGDOs engage it in practice. As observed through various perspectives from the literature and case studies, accountability is as problematic in its definition as it is in practice. A number of factors have contributed to the NGO accountability debate, including (but not limited to): growth of NGOs and their prominent role in service provision; increase in funding; NGOs seen as a voice of the voiceless; legitimacy; and democratization of development processes. Three models have been identified as reflecting NGO accountability: a) NGO accountability to patrons; b) NGO accountability to clients; and c) NGO accountability to themselves. In order to demonstrate accountability, NGDOs have used such tools as disclosure statements/reports; performance assessments; monitoring and evaluation; social audits; and certification. These tools are effective when used in an integrated manner rather than as discrete instruments. The chapter has argued that while the demand for accountability is a moral practice, the framework within which this debate unfolds is that of a "patron-client" relationship. This, by any means, calls for a rethink of the way in which accountability as a concept and its practical applications can be enhanced amidst competing interests among development stakeholders.

The moral crusade of fighting poverty is a journey that requires good leadership. Chapter 5 critically examined three concepts of leadership, management and governance, but the focus was on leadership. As observed throughout the chapter, leadership in NGDOs differs markedly from that of the corporate world, although there are many overlaps in the fundamental principles that govern both leadership and management. The nature of the development sector demands a different brand of leaders. Noting that communities in both the developing and developed countries are no longer the same as they were two decades ago, the debate in this chapter called for a redefinition of the idea of community due to the centrality of NGDOs in fostering change. Therefore, the chapter emphasized that for NGDOs, it is important that leadership development and nurturing should aim to facilitate collective leadership, collaborative leadership, steward leadership and many other forms of leadership which, in all cases, emphasize the type of leadership that crosses many boundaries: that is boundaries between organizations, groups and individuals. Importantly, NGDO leaders need leadership skills that deal with issues that divide communities. This is when the NGDO leaders need constantly to adapt to changing times. That said, we should also acknowledge that leadership is not about the "position" that a leader fills; rather it is about the behavior exhibited by those in positions of authority and how they relate to the rest of the people in the organization. Thus, NGDO leadership should learn to share power not only in their organizations but through ways in which the organizations are seen as vehicles or building blocks for community empowerment. Drawing on various case studies, the chapter highlighted the need for a reflective process where leaders can challenge their own assumptions, thereby encouraging adaptive, collective, serving and leading practices. The crux of the debate in this chapter was that NGDO leadership should facilitate processes in community development efforts where community leaders are encouraged to expand their perspectives from an emphasis on "I" to emphasizing both "I" and "we."

The linkage between leadership and learning became apparent in Chapter 6, where the idea of NGDOs as learning organizations was explored. Learning can mean different things to different people. While the definitions sound very simple, putting the ideas into practical application has proven a tricky business. The center of discussion in Chapter 6 was on reflection and relationship building. Besides this the chapter also highlighted that the most crucial aspect of learning in NGDOs rests in undemanding relations and how these relationships are essential building blocks to learning. However, this should be done with a conscious view of competing power dynamics in respective communities. The chapter noted that there are layers of power in those communities such that while NGDOs may take necessary steps to engage in learning at an organizational level, the milieu from which they draw their lessons is the community itself. As such, NGDO learning should have a balanced view in accommodating community and/or any indigenous knowledge. This is a conscious decision that has to be made and accommodated as part of a broader scheme that values learning as a conscious decision for change. From a project-based perspective, the chapter hinted that the use of monitoring and evaluation, as well as peer reviews, can truly enhance learning if these are done systematically with well-planned milestones. More importantly, this learning should transcend individual boundaries and be embedded into an organization so that it becomes an organizational culture.

Lessons: understanding poverty and why a crusade against poverty

The book has brought many lessons to the fore. Before highlighting these, we need to step back and rethink the idea of poverty. In one of the meetings I attended a few years back, one of the presenters, who is also a well known development critic, remarked: "To make poverty history, we need to understand the history of poverty." This statement has many crucial meanings in understanding development and its implications for ordinary people. One may even want to start by asking whether or not poverty does have a history. While volumes of books have been written on what poverty is, there is less articulation of why poverty exists and where it all started. While it is beyond the scope of this book, the global efforts to reduce poverty seem to pay less attention to why there is so much inequality; rather, attention is paid to dealing with poverty through, for example, the Millennium Development Goals (MDGs), which are explicit on what needs to be achieved but offer very little in terms of laying a solid background on why two-thirds of the world live in poverty and yet one-third of the global population lives in affluence.

Box 7.1 The Millennium Development Goals

1   Eradicate extreme poverty and hunger;
2   Achieve universal primary education;
3   Promote gender equality and empower women;
4   Reduce child mortality rates;
5   Improve maternal health;
6   Combat HIV/AIDS, malaria, and other diseases;

7 Ensure environmental sustainability; and
8 Develop a global partnership for development.
(United Nations, *Millennium Development Goals*, September 2000,
www.un.org/millenniumgoals/poverty.shtml)

For NGDOs, understanding the history of poverty helps them understand the global political economy of why, for example, inequality persists against over US$3 trillion spent in the name of development.[2] The legacy of colonialism (in the case of Africa and other parts of the developing world), and the extractive nature of some of the colonial and Western institutions, have left indelible imprints that impede efforts towards poverty reduction. As highlighted in the introductory chapter, the "charity model" espoused by the early civilizations was purely altruistic and rarely tackled the root causes of poverty and class struggle. The context within which the current NGDOs operate is predominantly defined by a poverty discourse of "lack of." For example, many definitions of poverty have focused on lack of materials, food, shelter and a few other basic needs, but have not delved deep into the structural causes of poverty.[3] To this end, there is a tendency to deal with the deficiencies as emergency stop-gap measures.

The relief that the "deficiency" approach offers has two sides. First it shows a moral duty which is operationalized in philanthropic and charity paradigms. The challenge before NGDOs is to go beyond these paradigms and delve deep into understanding social stratification and class struggle so that in doing so, the approach to poverty reduction shifts from band-aid to a beehive approach where NGDOs focus on advocating for, but at the same time providing, social services that are needed to reduce poverty. Crucially, the advocacy part of the approach has to be focused on dealing with structural issues that affect people's livelihoods. In other words, understanding the history of poverty is to understand how, today, poverty has been globalized in the new world order.[4] Therefore NGDOs' moral crusade can only be meaningful if there is a conscious effort to understand global social, political and economic injustices perpetrated by the global North to the global South.

Lesson 1: revisiting the aid debate and how NGDOs can manage it

The constant critique on the role of aid in development has its own platform in the current development discourse. As we noted in Chapter 1, aid, by its nature and the manner in which it is administered, is highly political. For the NGDO sector, the implications are far reaching. Do NGDOs bend to the whims of the donors, government or those that support them? Will succumbing to the demands of donors help accomplish a moral crusade of reducing poverty? These are not easy questions to answer given the current global aid architecture where the traditional donors (those from the North) are no longer in complete control of the current aid landscape.

Lately, the global South is bustling with an emerging economy comprising Brazil, Russia, India, China and South Africa (the BRICS), which, together with nations in the Arab world, are challenging the orthodoxy in the aid industry.[5] However, there is very little known about how these emerging donors deal with NGDOs. Within the current NGDO-donor relationships, the NGDO moral crusade in reducing poverty is under a constant test. This is especially vivid when one considers how accountability is handled. If the crusade is to alleviate poverty, then one would think that NGDOs' primary responsibility would be to their primary constituencies—their beneficiaries. This is rarely the case, as many of the case studies in this book have demonstrated.

Managing both "upwards" and "downwards" accountabilities in the aid debate is an issue that NGDOs can only address if they shift from dependency to self-sufficiency, particularly where they can demonstrate resourcefulness by harnessing local resources. For example, NGDOs can enter into small-scale entrepreneurial activities in order to raise funds to respond to development needs of their constituencies. This is not unusual. However, the challenge is that quite often it will require scaling up the programs to accommodate such strategies. By inference, the organization needs to build capacity to be able to deal with the demand and multiplicity of stakeholders with which to do business and at the same time manage its constituency.

Whatever the case may be, the NGDO sector has to rethink how it can graduate from the influence of donor conditionalities. In handling this, perhaps NGDOs need to heed a reminder from Fee, who aptly states:

> The schizophrenia which the dichotomy between their (NGDOs') role as agents of systemic change and their role as simply implementing agents for bilateral or multilateral donors may be part of the reason for their lack of effectiveness. It has been the search for funding outside the traditional national resources which has pushed NGOs into the aid delivery business.[6]

The point Fee raises is equally significant when we look at the nomenclature of "nongovernmental organizations." I have, on several occasions,[7] pointed out that NGDOs do not operate in a vacuum. Rather their work is complementary to what governments do in their quest for poverty reduction. For a while, the belief that NGOs are free from government influence has been delusional in the sense that the agenda to deal with poverty requires strategic alliances that are carefully entered into with respect to all stakeholders. The mandate for poverty alleviation still remains with governments whose endorsement through the ballot box legitimizes them as stewards of development. As such, the greatest challenge for NGDOs is to come to the realization that part of being free from donor influence is to harness national resources through collaborative efforts with government while at the same time paying attention to the politics of cooptation.

Lesson 2: the management of partnerships and capacity development issues

It is now becoming increasingly clear that the NGDO debate cannot escape the terms "partnership" and "capacity development." Despite their fluidity, these are terminologies that carry political baggage and the practical implications of which are far reaching and contestable. The various forms of partnership canvassed in this book are illustrative of the complex nature of the tension that exists between theory and practice. The critical question, the answer to which remains elusive, is: in whose benefit are all these types of partnerships? From the case studies, it can be noted that many of the partnerships are still loaded with imbalances of mutuality and trust.

It is apparent in the current global political economy that NGDOs' survival is at the mercy of other institutions, be those in the mainstream public domain or those in the market. Either way, the deployment of a particular form of partnership has to be dictated by a need rather than convenience. Hence, the models depicted by Gidron, Kramer and Salamon[8] and Tvedt[9] can be adopted and adapted to suit a particular need. The crucial aspect that needs to be borne in mind when debating partnerships between NGDOs and other stakeholders is that of power dynamics. Because of the fact that different NGDOs evolve differently and respond to needs according to their nature, the kinds of partnerships that have to be entered into need to be carefully thought out. Understanding the motives and interests of stakeholders helps shape the operations of such relationships. More importantly, it is a platform from which such entities can crucially draw the parameters within which issues of mutuality, respect and learning can be addressed.

The moral crusade NGDOs pursue in order to alleviate poverty has to be understood within competing power dynamics. To operate decisively, NGDOs not only require capacity in terms of skills development but also the ability to read and understand organizational structures and how these structures play in development processes. As highlighted in Chapter 6, many of the NGDOs are fortunate that they have grassroots contacts where critical development issues unfold. Their role is to utilize their presence and develop a culture where they become co-authors of knowledge through careful observation, deep reflection and the ability to interpret meanings from such information. It is this kind of engagement that NGDOs can manage to be instruments of social change.

The capacity development in NGDOs needs a radical shift from mere training to one that focuses on dealing with complexity.[10] As stated in previous sections, NGDOs operate in a complex social milieu full of tensions and contradictions as well as multiple realities. As such, it is highly essential that they develop systems that help them to:

- deal with the challenges and opportunities of working with multiple stakeholders and relationships;
- learn about development results;
- manage the challenges and opportunities of satisfying accountability and transparency issues; and
- deal with the challenges of strengthening the adaptive capacity of project and/or program stakeholders.[11]

Lesson 3: leadership and learning

It is perhaps clear from the case studies and a comprehensive review of literature in this book that the debate on NGDO leadership is still limited to the corporate world. Where it exists, it is rather sparse and the evidence is anecdotal. However, I would argue that in order to achieve positive results in their moral crusade, NGDO leaders need to be instrumental in engaging their members of staff and their beneficiaries in a process where information gathering, analysis and interpretation become part of the organizational and development culture. This does not happen unless the organization has the skills and capacity to be able to plan, monitor and evaluate any development interventions. Moreover, it is also in this context that field staff members develop critical thinking through individual, group and collective learning. The unpredictability of development processes can be very challenging not only to emerging NGDO but also to those that are fully established. Foley[12] proposes a range of mechanisms to help NGDO staff develop critical thinking and facilitation in a development process. These include, but are not limited to:

- a peer-supported and peer-facilitated community meeting where, at the end of the session, other members of staff can review the process and contribute to how such activities could be improved;
- regular team days where members of staff in an organization discuss and debate development issues with feedback from members of the organization;
- external members of a development organization acting as mentors to junior staff of another organization with the view to maximize learning and development approaches—cross-institutional mentoring that helps avoid personality clashes and internal politicking;
- inter-institutional peer learning processes where the sharing of experiences is encouraged. This can take the form of community-based organizations interacting with INGOs;
- mutual academic-NGO occasional conversation series where the academy and development practitioners share issues on how theory translates into practice;
- INGO and local partner staff engaging in role-reversal exercises in which, for example, each has an opportunity to experience (capacity-building/partnership) situations from the other point of view;
- sharing of case studies of both challenging as well as successful interventions and allowing members of the organization in collaboration with other NGDOs, both local or international, to reflect on and discuss various solutions to such case scenarios; and
- peer review of programs and projects.[13]

More needs to be done

The book has provided a platform to rethink the future of NGDOs in their development endeavors. While indeed there is an intense debate on the notions of aid effectiveness, aid and development partnerships, capacity building and/or development, accountability, transparency, sustainability and many more, there is a lack of evidence on how all these ideas are unfolding in practice. With limited exposition of case studies on these notions in this book, it is therefore undeniably crucial that more research be done to uncover the practicalities of these ideas. The following research could be undertaken:

- The dynamics of government. NGDO partnerships where NGDOs are subcontracted to implement government development programs. The idea of "subcontracting" in the context where NGDOs are still clinging to "nongovernmental" identity needs more understanding.
- The role of leadership in NGDOs in enhancing the achievement of MDGs. While there is a lot of talk about poverty falling and, with the obvious contribution the NGDO sector makes, it would be vital to draw lessons on the extent to which part of the success in the story is attributed to leadership, management or the governance of development organizations.
- Success stories of NGDO accountability. From a few sporadic cases on NGO corruption, one is left wondering how grave this challenge is in development organizations. This is the heart of the matter of the theme of this book. The major question we could explore is in what ways do NGDOs manage and account resources to their beneficiaries "downwards"?
- How and in what ways do NGDO projects funded by traditional Western donors differ from those funded by the BRICS? What lessons can be drawn from such a study in relation to the effects of conditionalities, accountability, management and effectiveness?

Final thought

There are grounds for continued optimism despite the odds. The NGDO sector is a phenomenon that holds the potential for a significant contribution to the development field. Probably it is time to heed Jeremy Hobbs, the executive director of Oxfam International, who said "Development is increasingly about political alliances and action, rather than service delivery, technical projects and large grants."[14]

Notes

1 Nikolas Barry-Shaw and Dru O. Jay, *Paved with Good Intentions: Canada's Development NGOs from Idealism to Imperialism* (Halifax, N.C. and Winnipeg: Fernwood Publishing, 2012).
2 Dambisa Moyo, *Dead Aid: Why Aid is Not Working and How there is a Better Way for Africa* (New York: Farrar, Straus and Giroux, 2009).
3 Pete Alcock, *Understanding Poverty*, 2nd edn (Basingstoke: Macmillan Press, 1997).
4 Michael Chossudovsky, *The Globalization of Poverty and the New World Order*, 2nd edn (Pincourt, Quebec: Global Research-Centre for Research on Globalization, 2003).
5 Lindsay Whitfield, "Reframing the Aid Debate: Why Aid isn't Working and How it Should be Changed," *DISS Working Paper 2009:34*

(Copenhagen: Danish Institute for International Studies, 2009), www.diis. dk/graphics/publications/wp2009/wp2009-34_refraiming_the_aid_debate. pdf; Julie Walz and Vijaya Ramachandran, "Brave New World: A Literature Review of Emerging Donors and the Changing Nature of Foreign Assistance," Centre for Global Development, Working Paper 273 (November 2011), www.cgdev.org/files/1425691_file_Walz_Ramachandran_Brave_New _World_FINAL.pdf.

6 Derek Fee, *How to Manage an Aid Exit Strategy: The Future of Development Aid* (London: Zed Books, 2012).

7 Jonathan J. Makuwira, "Non-Governmental Organizations (NGOs) and Participatory Development in Basic Education in Malawi," *Current Issues in Comparative Education* 6, no. 2 (2004), www.tc.columbia.edu/cice/article s/jm162.htm; Jonathan J. Makuwira, "Civil Society Organizations (CSOs) and the Changing Nature of African Politics: The Case of the CSO– Government Relationship in Malawi," *Journal of Asian and African Studies* 46, no. 6 (2011): 615–28.

8 Benjamin Gidron, Ralph Kramer and Lester Salamon, "Government and the Third Sector in Comparative Perspective: Allies or Adversaries?" in *Government and the Third Sector: Emerging Relationships in Welfare States*, ed. Benjamin Gidron, Ralph Kramer and Lester Salamon (San Francisco, Calif.: Jossey-Bass Publishers, 1992).

9 Terje Tvedt, *Angels of Mercy or Development Diplomats? NGOs and Foreign Aid* (Trenton, N.J.: African World Press, 1998).

10 Jan V. Ongevalle, Anneke Maarse, Cristien Temmink, Eugenia Boutylkova and Huib Huyse, "Dealing with Complexity through Planning, Monitoring and Evaluation (PME): Mid-Term Results of a Collaborative Action Research Process," INTRAC Praxis Paper 26 (January 2012), www.intrac. org/data/files/resources/736/Praxis-Paper-26-Dealing-with-complexity-through -PME.pdf.

11 Ongevalle *et al.*, "Dealing with Complexity through Planning, Monitoring and Evaluation (PME)."

12 Connell Foley, "Developing Critical Thinking in NGO Field Staff," *Development in Practice* 18, no. 6 (2008): 774–78.

13 Foley, "Developing Critical Thinking in NGO Field Staff," 766–77.

14 Jeremy Hobbs, "Responding to Complexity and Change: Oxfam International's Approach," *Ontrac* 54 (May 2013): 3, www.intrac.org/data/files/ resources/769/ONTRAC-54-The-rise-of-INGO-families.pdf.

Select bibliography

Nikolas Barry-Smith and Dru Oja Jay, *Paved with Good Intentions: Canada's Development NGOs from Idealism to Imperialism* (Halifax, N.C.: Fernwood Publishing, 2012). This book is a new entry on the development scene. The authors unmask the subtleties of development NGOs which, in the broader scheme of things, are constantly accused of propagating neoliberal agendas of the Western hegemony. A great resource that cuts through the foggy debate about the role of international aid agencies.

Jen Bendell, *Debating NGO Accountability* (New York: UN Non-Governmental Liaison Service, 2006). An incredible resource that provides an in-depth analysis of NGOs and accountability issues. The text advances the accountability debate raised by such theorists as Michael Edwards and David Hulme in their seminal work *NGO Performance and Accountability: Beyond the Magic Bullet.*

Alan Fowler, *Striking a Balance: A Guide to Enhancing the Effectiveness of Non-Governmental Organizations in International Development* (London: Earthscan, 1997). An important piece of work which offers a comprehensive examination of people-centered development and how development NGOs can enhance their effectiveness and impact. It provides a compelling case for pragmatism and how NGOs can realize their vision. This is a very useful reference for practitioners in the development field.

Alan Fowler and Chiku W. Malunga, eds, *NGO Management: The Earthscan Companion* (London: Earthscan, 2010). An edited volume containing scholarly analysis of NGO management and leadership. It offers new perspectives on issues of NGO effectiveness, advocacy, social movements, knowledge management and other pressing development debates in the new globalized world.

Hans Holmén, *Snakes in Paradise: NGOs and the Aid Industry in Africa* (Sterling, Va.: Kumarian Press, 2010). This book offers an insightful argument about the role of NGOs in Africa. In particular, it critiques development approaches undertaken by NGOs working in Africa and cautions against generalized conclusions about NGOs as alternative instruments to Africa's development trajectory.

David Lewis and Nazneen Kanji, *Non-Governmental Organisations and Development* (London: Routledge, 2009). This book provides a comprehensive overview of the role of NGOs in development, highlighting the theory and practice of development and how NGOs can make a contribution.

Jonathan Makuwira, "Development? Freedom? Whose Development and Freedom?" *Development in Practice* 16, no. 2 (2006): 193–200. This article explains how NGOs claim the moral high ground and ignore the essence of participatory development. For readers interested in understanding practical development issues, the journal *Development in Practice* is recommended.

NGO Café, www.gdrc.org/ngo. A very useful virtual library on nongovernmental organizations. It was set up as a think tank for NGOs to discuss issues of critical importance to development. The site contains numerous links to websites which are very useful in the development field, in particular NGOs, and development in general.

Paul Ronalds, *The Change Imperative: Creating the Next Generation NGO* (Sterling, Va.: Kumarian Press, 2010). This book offers an analysis of how current global and/or international politics is shaping the role and influence of international NGOs. It is an invaluable resource for understanding international NGOs in a globalized world.

Jan Ubels, Naa-Aku Acquaye-Baddoo, and Alan Fowler, eds, *Capacity Development in Practice* (London: Earthscan, 2010). A collection of essays on capacity development. The volume contains essays inspiring enough to stimulate a critical reflection on the tensions and contradictions inherent in the notion of capacity development, and highlights how NGOs can engage their constituencies in supporting development initiatives.

Index

Routledge Global Institutions Series

UNICEF
by Richard Jolly (University of Sussex)

International Migration
by Khalid Koser (Geneva Centre for Security Policy)

Human Development
by Richard Ponzio

The International Monetary Fund (2nd edition)
Politics of conditional lending
by James Raymond Vreeland (Georgetown University)

The UN Global Compact
by Catia Gregoratti (Lund University)

Institutions for Women's Rights
*by Charlotte Patton (York College, CUNY) and
Carolyn Stephenson (University of Hawaii)*

International Aid
by Paul Mosley (University of Sheffield)

Global Consumer Policy
by Karsten Ronit (University of Copenhagen)

The Changing Political Map of Global Governance
*by Anthony Payne (University of Sheffield) and
Stephen Robert Buzdugan (Manchester Metropolitan University)*

Coping with Nuclear Weapons
by W. Pal Sidhu

Private Foundations and Development Partnerships
by Michael Moran (Swinburne University of Technology)

The International Politics of Human Rights
*edited by Monica Serrano (Colegio de Mexico) and
Thomas G. Weiss (The CUNY Graduate Center)*

Twenty-First-Century Democracy Promotion in the Americas
*by Jorge Heine (The Centre for International Governance Innovation) and
Brigitte Weiffen (University of Konstanz)*

EU Environmental Policy and Climate Change
by Henrik Selin (Boston University) and
Stacy VanDeveer (University of New Hampshire)

Making Global Institutions Work
Power, accountability and change
edited by Kate Brennan

The Society for Worldwide Interbank Financial
Telecommunication (SWIFT)
by Susan Scott (London School of Economics and
Political Science) and Markos Zachariadis (University of Cambridge)

Global Governance and China
The dragon's learning curve
edited by Scott Kennedy (Indiana University)

The Politics of Global Economic Surveillance
by Martin S. Edwards (Seton Hall University)

Mercy and Mercenaries
Humanitarian agencies and private security companies
by Peter Hoffman

Regional Organizations in the Middle East
by James Worrall (University of Leeds)

Reforming the UN Development System
The politics of incrementalism
by Silke Weinlich (Duisburg-Essen University)

Post-2015 UN Development
Making change happen
by Stephen Browne (FUNDS Project) and
Thomas G. Weiss (CUNY Graduate Center)

Who Participates?
States, bureaucracies, NGOs and global governance
by Molly Anne Ruhlman

The United Nations as a Knowledge Organization
by Nanette Svenson (Tulane University)

United Nations Centre on Transnational Corporations (UNCTC)
by Khalil Hamdani and Lorraine Ruffing

The International Criminal Court
The politics and practice of prosecuting atrocity crimes
by Martin Mennecke (University of Copenhagen)

For further information regarding the series, please contact:
Craig Fowlie, Publisher, Politics & International Studies
Taylor & Francis
2 Park Square, Milton Park, Abingdon
Oxford OX14 4RN, UK
+44 (0)207 842 2057 Tel
+44 (0)207 842 2302 Fax
Craig.Fowlie@tandf.co.uk
www.routledge.com